D1530877

Write Right!

Rewrite Right!

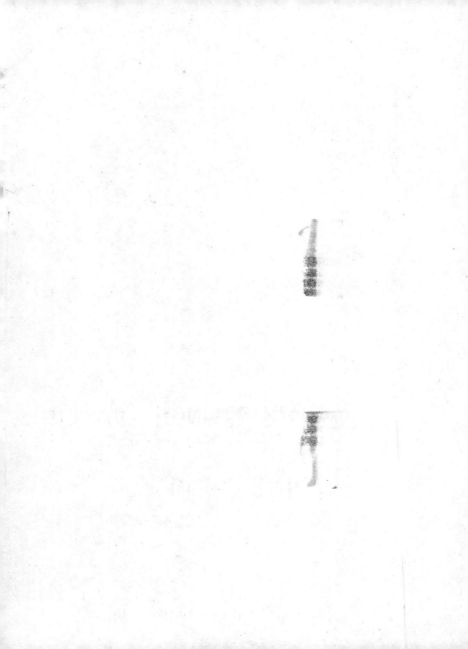

Write Right!

A Desktop Digest of Punctuation, Grammar, and Style

Rewrite Right!

JAN VENOLIA

TEN SPEED PRESS
Berkeley | Toronto

This special edition published exclusively for Barnes & Noble, Inc.,
by Ten Speed Press.

Cover design by Katy Brown, based on a design by Paul Kepple
Book design by Tasha Hall
Copyediting by Suzanne Byerley
Illustrations by Ellen Sasaki
Excerpt from a Donella Meadows column on pp. 59–60 (Rewrite Right!) was first
published in The Global Citizen, December 18, 1999. Reprinted with permission.

ISBN-13: 978-1-4351-0646-8

Printed in Canada
First printing this edition, 2008

1 2 3 4 5 6 7 8 9 10 — 12 11 10 09 08

Write
Right!

> *Words are the only tools you will be given.*
> *Learn to use them with originality and care.*
> *Value them for their strength and diversity.*
> *And also remember that somebody*
> *out there is listening.*
> —William Zinsser
>
> *Amen.*
> —Jan Venolia

Contents

Why All the Fuss?

> *Our language is an invaluable resource,*
> *as much a part of our heritage as forests,*
> *wildlife, and waters.*—Paul Lovinger

Does good writing matter any more? In an e-commerce environment, do you still need to know how to create an effective sentence? Absolutely! Magazines, newspapers, and books are written words, whether in electronic or print form. What emerges from fax machines and appears on computer screens is writing, not speech. Businesses still need to "put it in writing." Furthermore, what's written needs to be clear and concise. That's where punctuation and grammar come in.

On the job or at school, you probably have to write—fast *and* well. You need to know how to choose the words that best convey your ideas and how to organize them for maximum effect. Can you rely on software to improve your writing? It helps. You can easily revise text, experiment with format, and find typos (though spell-checkers have definite limitations). But grammar-checkers are more annoying than useful. A concise handbook like *Write Right!* remains your best bet.

But what *is* good writing? And who says so? Who decides which changes in language are acceptable and which are to be rejected? Described as "usage wars," this subject is hotly debated in language and education circles.

On one side, the combatants declare that what constitutes good English should not be determined by arbitrary and archaic rules but by how the language has evolved. They cite the living nature of language to justify accepting change of all kinds. They study everyday speech and writing, and what they determine to be the norms are then deemed acceptable. Anyone who disagrees is considered to be elitist.

Trying to hold the line against this "anything goes" approach are those who believe that effective communication adheres to certain rules. Those rules make it more likely that written words will be understood. Clear writing is not seen as "archaic" but just good policy.

By now, you have probably deduced which side I'm on in these language wars. I, in turn, am able to make some assumptions about you. You are reading these lines, so I presume you want sound guidance in the matter of writing well.

I will not advise you that the language you hear on the street or even on the evening news is what you should emulate. Instead, I will draw upon judgments accumulated over decades of writing, of reading, and of studying the rules of clear and effective writing.

My judgments are grounded in the belief that making the reader's job easier is in the interests of reader and writer alike.

By making the reader's job easier, you show respect. You show consideration. At the same time, you improve the odds of being understood and thus of communicating what you want to communicate. True, an ill-formed, confusing sentence can usually be teased apart and understood—eventually. But why waste the reader's time trying to guess what you mean? Clarity and precision are always desirable.

Be forewarned, while you're improving your writing, I want you to rediscover the English language and rally to its defense. Its richness and variety are under siege. When *disinterested* becomes synonymous with *uninterested* and *dilemma* with *predicament*, we lose important tools for expressing ourselves. If wrong words proliferate, then *hone* replaces *home*, *staunch* crowds out *stanch*, and we encounter hybrids like *doubtlessly*, a kissing cousin of the redundant *irregardless*. Theodore Bernstein, author of *The Careful Writer*, suggests that accepting this degradation of language is the equivalent of declaring a crime legal when it has been committed often enough.

Concerned about this loss of richness in our language, I've expanded the sections on usage and style in *Write Right!* Alas, many of the examples of errors that I've included come from magazines, newspapers, and even books—publications that had been read by someone who was paid to catch such errors. Even so, the best antidote for the epidemic of wrong words is to read widely but with an informed eye. I propose to help you become informed.

Write Right! covers the common errors writers make in punctuation and grammar. Avoiding those errors means you're off to a good start. But lifeless prose and sloppy usage are greater threats to good writing than misuse of an apostrophe, so the rest of the book addresses those problems as well.

PART ONE, *The Basics*, provides a review of grammatical terms. Though not ends in themselves, the terms do help you understand the rules I've included in this book. Chapter 1, "Coming to Terms with Terms," defines the eight parts of speech and describes the elements that make up sentences. It goes into additional detail for the two trickiest parts of speech, verbs and pronouns.

PART TWO, *The Tools of Writing*, covers grammar, punctuation, and copyediting. Refer to Chapter 2, "Grammatical Guidelines," with questions about agreement of subject and verb or how to avoid dangling modifiers. Chapter 3, "Punctuation Pointers," tells you where to put apostrophes and commas, while Chapter 4, "Copyediting Considerations," helps you add a professional gloss in such matters as capitalization, italics, and treatment of numbers.

PART THREE, *The Craft of Writing*, considers the final product. Chapter 5, "Words," takes a look at the words we use and how we use them. Its list of tricky words sorts out confusing pairs like *affect* and *effect* and brings you up to date on the acceptability of such words as *contact* and *hopefully*. Chapter 6, "Style," helps you root out ho-hum writing. After all, a sentence can be grammatically correct, properly punctuated, and still be tedious. You want to invigorate your writing as well.

The final section in the book, *Resources*, includes a glossary, bibliography, list of frequently misspelled words, and the addresses of some interesting Web sites.

As in previous editions of *Write Right!*, the rules are illustrated with quotations that were chosen to edify and amuse. Throughout, Ellen Sasaki's whimsical drawings keep us from taking ourselves, and our rules, too seriously.

Write Right! answers the questions about writing that come up most often in your work or studies. Keep it next to your keyboard or tucked in a desk drawer for ready reference. If you need help with a more advanced level of revising, refer to *Rewrite Right! Your Guide to Perfectly Polished Prose*. (See the bibliography.)

The more you practice good writing, the easier it becomes. Enjoy the process!

> *By our choices we make usage, good or bad. Let us then try to make good choices, and guard and praise our lovely language and try to be worthy of her.*—Morris Bishop

Writing is easy. All you have to do is
cross out the wrong words.
—Mark Twain

Part One
The Basics

1 Coming to Terms with Terms

> *Words are all we have.*
> —Samuel Beckett

Recently, a friend was fretting that she didn't remember what predicates were. I assured her that you don't have to be able to define a grammatical term in order to use it correctly. Terminology is just a tool—a handy way to refer to the elements of writing. It's a lot easier to say "predicate" than "a word or group of words that makes a statement or asks a question about the subject of a sentence."

If you have only a few holes in your grammar vocabulary, skip this chapter now and refer to it as needed. But if you want a thorough review of grammatical terms, begin right here.

Parts of Speech

Let's start by defining the eight parts of speech: noun, verb, adjective, adverb, conjunction, preposition, pronoun, and interjection. Then we'll look at how they function in sentences.

Noun: *n.*, a word that names a person, place, thing, quality, or act.

> The <u>wise</u> talk because they have something to say; <u>fools</u> because they have to say something.—Plato

 If you can put *a*, *an*, or *the* in front of a word, it's a noun.

Proper nouns identify specific persons, places, or things.

> Taj Mahal, Halloween, Aristotle, Cairo, Titanic

Common nouns are ordinary, run-of-the-mill nouns.

> kitten, bravery, shoelace, letter, honesty

Nouns can be concrete (*toenail, tinsel, tomahawk*) or abstract (*duty, diligence, danger*).

Verb: *v.*, a word that expresses action (*to win*), occurrence (*to happen*), or mode of being (*am, was, are* and the other forms of *to be*).

> You <u>climb</u> a long ladder until you <u>see</u> over the roof, or over the clouds. You <u>are writing</u> a book.—Annie Dillard

A sentence isn't complete without a verb, so it's important to be able to recognize them. (See p. 12.)

Helping verbs (also called **auxiliary verbs**) save you the trouble of changing the main verb to show past, present, and future tense. The twenty-three helping verbs are *can, could, would, should, do, does, did, has, have, had, may, might,* *must, shall,* and *will* plus the eight forms of *to be* (*am, are, be, been, being, is, was, were*).

> In what other language <u>could</u> your nose run and your feet smell.—Richard Lederer

> <u>May</u> your left ear wither and fall into your right pocket. —Ancient curse

Linking verbs, as their name suggests, provide the connection between the subject and the noun or adjective in the predicate.

> Opportunities always <u>look</u> bigger going than coming.

Pronoun: *pron.,* a word that takes the place of a noun. Examples are *they, it, you, who,* and *she.*

> <u>It</u>'s so beautifully arranged on the plate, <u>you</u> know that <u>someone</u>'s fingers have been all over <u>it</u>.—Julia Child

> Experience is a wonderful thing. <u>It</u> enables <u>you</u> to recognize a mistake when <u>you</u> see <u>it</u> again.

What the pronoun replaces is called its **antecedent.** Pronouns are particularly helpful if the antecedent is long or complicated: leftover macaroni and cheese; an inner-city after-school program; a dense, nutty-flavored, unassuming wine.

Adjective: *adj.,* a word or group of words that modifies a noun or pronoun.

> <u>purple</u> possum, <u>hysterical</u> hippopotamus, <u>slimy</u> salamander

Adjectives are called modifiers because they limit or restrict the words they are modifying. Not just any possum, but the *purple* possum.

> *Bad* times have a *scientific* value; these are occasions a *good* learner would not miss.—Ralph Waldo Emerson

The adjectives *a*, *an*, and *the* are called **articles.** When you see an article, you know that a noun is coming.

Adverb: *adv.*, a word or group of words that modifies a verb, adjective, or other adverb. Adverbs answer such questions as when (*now*), where (*aloft*), how much (*very*), to what extent (*extremely*), and in what manner (*deftly*).

Both adjectives and adverbs are modifiers, but they modify different kinds of words. Adjectives modify nouns or pronouns; adverbs modify verbs, adjectives, or other adverbs.

Age is a <u>very</u> <u>high</u> <u>price</u> to pay for maturity.
       adv.   adj.   noun

The adverb *very* modifies the adjective *high*; the adjective *high* modifies the noun *price*.

Conjunction: *conj.*, a word that connects other words, phrases, and clauses.

peaches <u>and</u> cream   shaken <u>but</u> not stirred

Coordinating conjunctions (*and, but, or, nor, for, so, yet*) connect terms of equal grammatical value.

Blessed are they who can laugh at themselves <u>for</u> they shall never cease to be amused.

Correlative conjunctions are coordinating conjunctions that come in pairs: *either/or, not only/but also, both/and, whether/or*.

I figure you have the same chance of winning the lottery <u>whether</u> you play <u>or</u> not.—Fran Lebowitz

Publishing literary novels is like sailing a small craft; <u>either</u> you catch the wind <u>or</u> you paddle very hard.—Nan Talese

Subordinating conjunctions connect clauses of unequal grammatical value: an independent and a dependent clause. An independent clause can stand by itself as a complete sentence; a dependent clause requires an independent clause to complete its meaning. Subordinating conjunctions include *until, since, before, as, if, when, although, because, as long as,* and *after*.

<u>If</u> you look like your passport picture, you probably need the trip.

Always yield to temptation, <u>because</u> it may not pass by your way again.

Preposition: *prep.*, a word that shows the relationship between its object (the noun or pronoun following the preposition) and other words in a sentence.

The most common prepositions show direction (*through* the looking glass), time (*during* her term of office), and possession (*with* my friends). Less obvious examples of prepositions include *notwithstanding, concerning,* and *in spite of*. If a word shows the relation of a noun or pronoun to another word in the sentence, it's a preposition.

A balanced diet is a cookie <u>in</u> each hand.

A **prepositional phrase** consists of the preposition plus its object and any modifiers of the object.

The only time the world beats a path <u>to my door</u> is when I'm <u>in the bathroom</u>.

Perhaps no other rule of grammar has prompted so many to say so much as the now-outdated rule prohibiting ending a sentence with a preposition.

The grammar has a rule absurd
Which I would call an outworn myth:
A preposition is a word
You mustn't end a sentence with.
　　　　　　　　—Berton Braley

It is, indeed, an outworn myth.

Interjection: *interj.*, a word or phrase that conveys strong emotion or surprise; an exclamation.

Heavens, Maude!　Help!　Never!　Oops!　Cool!

The Elements of a Sentence

When the parts of speech are used in a sentence, we give them new names: subject, predicate, object, complement, and modifier.

Subject: Who or what the sentence is about.

If you put *Who?* or *What?* in front of a verb, your answer is the subject.

> <u>*An investment in knowledge*</u> *always pays the best interest.*—Benjamin Franklin

What pays the best interest? An investment in knowledge.

A **simple subject** does not include any modifiers.

> A <u>conscience</u> is what hurts when all your other parts feel good.

A **complete subject** is the simple subject plus all the words that modify it.

> <u>*Constant dripping*</u> *hollows out a stone.*—Lucretius

> <u>Someone who thinks logically</u> provides a nice contrast to the real world.

> <u>*The best part of fiction in many novels*</u> *is the notice that the characters are purely imaginary.*—Franklin P. Adams

A **compound subject** is two or more simple subjects.

> <u>*Banks and riches*</u> *are chains of gold, but still chains.* —Edmund Ruffin

> <u>*Directors, coaches, and editors*</u> *cannot teach you how to get there. But they can put you on the paths that* lead there. —Thomas McCormack

Predicate: Everything in the sentence that isn't the subject.

A predicate explains or describes what the subject is doing.

> *A Canadian is someone who knows how to make love in a*
> subject   predicate
> *canoe.*—Pierre Berton

A **simple predicate** is synonymous with the verb.

> Bills <u>travel</u> through the mail at twice the speed of checks.

> A closed mouth <u>gathers</u> no feet.

A **complete predicate** includes verbs, objects, modifiers, and complements.

> Bills <u>travel through the mail at twice the speed of checks</u>.

> A closed mouth <u>gathers no feet</u>.

A **compound predicate** is two or more predicates with the same subject.

> *A poem <u>begins</u> in delight and <u>ends</u> in wisdom.*
> —Robert Frost

> *When we read, we <u>start</u> at the beginning and <u>continue</u> until we reach the end; when we write, we <u>start</u> in the middle and <u>fight</u> our way out.*—Vickie Karp

A subject or predicate is said to be *understood* if it is not actually stated but is clearly implied.

> <u>Eat</u> well, <u>stay</u> fit, <u>die</u> anyway. (The understood subject is **you**.)

Object: (1) A noun that receives or is affected by the action of the verb; (2) the noun following a preposition.

I would certainly go to the <u>barricades</u> for any <u>movement</u> that wants to sweep away the <u>Pentagon, Time magazine, and frozen french-fried potatoes</u>.—Gore Vidal

Barricades is the object of the preposition *to*, and *movement* is the object of the preposition *for*. *Pentagon*, Time *magazine*, and *frozen french-fried potatoes* are objects of the verb *sweep*.

A **direct object** answers the question *What?* or *Whom?* after the verb.

I hit the <u>wall</u>.	I greeted <u>Analisa</u>.
direct obj.	direct obj.

An **indirect object** receives the direct object.

I gave <u>Analisa</u> a <u>hug</u>.
    indirect   direct
      obj.   obj.

Complement: A word or phrase that completes the meaning of the verb.

Make <u>my day</u>.

Clem and Maude are learning to dance <u>the tango</u>.

Genius is <u>one percent inspiration and ninety-nine percent perspiration</u>.—Thomas A. Edison

Too many pieces finish <u>long after the end</u>.—Igor Stravinsky

Modifier: Words that describe or limit other words (see Adjective, Adverb).

<u>apple</u> pie   <u>friendly</u> advice   <u>printed</u> statement

The most successful politician is he *who says what everybody is thinking most often and in the loudest voice*.
—Theodore Roosevelt

Be careful not to misplace modifiers (see p. 39) or let them dangle (see p. 40).

Putting the Pieces Together

Sentences are made up of phrases and clauses. A **phrase** has no subject or predicate; it can serve as different parts of speech.

Prepositional phrase: under the gun

Gerund phrase: knowing the answer

Noun phrase: a nation of more than five million people

A **clause** has a subject and predicate. Clauses that express a complete thought are called **independent**; they can stand alone. Clauses that do not express a complete thought are called **dependent**; they cannot stand alone.

By the time you can make ends meet, they move the ends.
        dependent clause   independent clause

What makes a sentence a **sentence**? A subject, a predicate, and a complete thought. Anything short of a complete thought is a **fragment.**

Fragment: While I was looking at the sunset.

Complete Sentence: While I was looking at the sunset, I drove into a tree.

Used wisely, a fragment is an effective device. It provides emphasis, answers a question, or introduces a change of pace.

However, the reader should never feel that something is missing or that you just tacked on an afterthought.

A **simple sentence** consists of an independent clause.

> *Justice delayed is justice denied.*—William Gladstone

> *Too much of a good thing can be wonderful.*—Mae West

A **compound sentence** consists of two or more independent clauses; they are joined by a coordinating conjunction or a semicolon.

> *A little learning is a dangerous thing, but a lot of ignorance is just as bad.*—Bob Edwards

> *I was thirty-two when I started cooking; up until then, I just ate.*—Julia Child

A **complex sentence** consists of a dependent and an independent clause.

> *Even if you're on the right track, you'll get run over if you just sit there.*—Will Rogers
>   dependent clause   independent clause

There are four more ways to classify sentences.

- DECLARATIVE: Makes a statement

  Nothing so denies a person liberty as the total absence of money.—John Kenneth Galbraith

- INTERROGATIVE: Asks a question

  Was it Frank Lloyd Wright who described television as chewing gum for the eyes?

If I counted the pages I've torn up, of how many volumes am I the author?—Colette

- IMPERATIVE: Gives an order or makes a request

  Put all your eggs in one basket—and watch that basket!
  —Mark Twain

  Fill what's empty. Empty what's full. Scratch where it itches.—Alice Roosevelt Longworth

- EXCLAMATORY: Expresses a strong emotion

  Dear God, I pray for patience. And I want it right now!
  —Oren Arnold

More About Verbs

Verbs have different forms. By changing the form of a verb, you provide the following information:

- Number
- Person
- Voice
- Tense
- Mood

Number shows if a word is *singular* (only one of something) or *plural* (more than one).

> she waltzes, he waltzes, *but* they waltz (*not* they waltzes)

Person tells who is the speaker (first person), who is spoken to (second person), and who is spoken about (third person). Person determines which verb and pronoun to use.

Voice shows whether the subject of the verb is acting (**active voice**) or being acted upon (**passive voice**).

Active voice: Celeste is assembling a computer.

Passive voice: The computer is being assembled by Celeste.

Tense tells when an action is happening: in the present (now), in the future, or in the past. As you can see in the table below, sometimes the main verb uses a helping verb to show tense.

SINGULAR	PRESENT	PAST	FUTURE
1st Person	I dance	I danced	I will dance
2nd Person	you dance	you danced	you will dance
3rd Person	he, she, it dances	he, she, it danced	he, she, it will dance

PLURAL	PRESENT	PAST	FUTURE
1st Person	we dance	we danced	we will dance
2nd Person	you dance	you danced	you will dance
3rd Person	they dance	they danced	they will dance

Mood can be considered as verbs with an attitude. Is the attitude matter-of-fact, commanding, or hypothetical? These three categories translate into the indicative, imperative, and subjunctive moods, respectively.

We use the **indicative mood** for statements of fact or questions about facts (*The dish ran away with the spoon*). We use the **imperative mood** to give commands (*Listen to me*) and to present instructions *(Place the petri dish in the sterilizer)*. Most writing is in the indicative or imperative, and using these moods is pretty automatic. But you may need a little guidance with the subjunctive.

The **subjunctive mood** conveys situations that are hypothetical, doubtful, or even contrary to fact *(If it were true...)*. Like the woman who was surprised to learn she had been speaking prose all her life, you may be unaware that you've been using the subjunctive every time you say "I wish I were rich."(For most of us, that's a condition contrary to fact.)

The New York Public Library Writer's Guide has a helpful description of the subjunctive.

> The subjunctive mood can seem like speaking English in a slightly different universe, where the basic rules of tense are reversed: Present tense is used for past, past is used for present, and *be* is used for *is, am*, and *are*.

The following examples illustrate where and how to use the subjunctive.

- An improbable condition or one that is contrary to fact

  If I <u>were</u> you, I wouldn't jump out of that airplane.

  If pregnancy <u>were</u> a book, they would cut the last two chapters.—Nora Ephron

  He spoke of his idea as if it <u>were</u> a complete solution.

- An indirect command

  The postal clerk insisted that the return address <u>be</u> included.

His piano teacher suggested that he <u>practice</u> more often.

- Motions and resolutions

   I move that the meeting <u>be</u> adjourned.

   Resolved, that my birthday <u>be</u> declared a national holiday.

Verb Forms (Verbals)

When verbs act like nouns, adjectives, or adverbs, they are called **infinitives, gerunds,** and **participles.**

Infinitives combine a verb and the word *to* (*to write, to speak*). Infinitives can act as adverbs, adjectives, or nouns.

   As an adverb: I struggled <u>to fly</u> despite the strong winds.

The infinitive *to fly* modifies the verb *struggled*.

   As a noun: <u>To fly</u> to Honolulu is my dream.

The infinitive *to fly* is the subject of the verb *is*.

   As an adjective: For a real thrill, the place <u>to fly</u> is Rio de Janeiro.

The infinitive *to fly* modifies the noun *place*.

You create a **split infinitive** when you put a word between the verb and *to*, as in *to steadily increase* or *to boldly go*. Split infinitives have a long history of being acceptable and only a brief interlude of being frowned upon. Today, language authorities agree: If a split infinitive improves readability, split away.

   We expect the advantages to more than compensate for the cost.

Gerunds are verbs that end in *-ing* and perform the job of nouns.

> <u>Playing</u> bridge <u>takes</u> concentration.
> gerund   verb

The main verb in this sentence is *takes*, not *playing*. The gerund *playing* is part of the complete subject: *playing bridge*. As a subject, it is doing the job of a noun.

> *<u>Thinking</u> is the hardest work there is, which is probably why so few people do it.*—Henry Ford

> *I don't think <u>living</u> in cellars and <u>starving</u> is any better for an artist than it is for anybody else.*—Katherine Anne Porter

> *Imagine <u>straddling</u> the cosmos, <u>clinging</u> to the tails of comets, <u>knowing</u> that time does not exist.*—Erica Jong

Participles are forms of the verb that either serve as an adjective or show tense.

- Participles acting as adjectives end in *ing*, *en*, *d*, *ed*, or *t*.

  swoll<u>en</u> toe   burn<u>ing</u> question   miss<u>ed</u> opportunity

- Participles that show tense vary according to the verb.

Regular verbs form the past tense and past participle by adding *d* or *ed* to the present tense.

Present Tense	Past Tense	Past Participle
dine	dined	dined
dream	dreamed	dreamed
invent	invented	invented

Irregular verbs change other letters or become an entirely different word in the past tense and past participle.

Present Tense	Past Tense	Past Participle
know	knew	known
shrink	shrank	shrunk
think	thought	thought

Participles need an auxiliary or helping verb to show tense.

I <u>might have</u> <u>thought</u> so.
    helping verb   participle

I <u>am</u> <u>thinking</u> about it.
helping participle
 verb

I <u>had</u> <u>thought</u> better of it.
helping participle
 verb

I <u>will be</u> <u>thinking</u> of them.
  helping   participle
    verb

A **participial phrase** combines a participle and its modifiers.

<u>The spaceship</u>, <u>lurching wildly</u>, <u>approached the runway</u>.
    subject   participial phrase   predicate

More About Pronouns

The five kinds of pronouns are personal, relative, indefinite, demonstrative, and interrogative. Pronouns are classified by how they are used in a sentence.

Personal pronouns replace nouns.

Singular: I, me, you, he, him, she, her, it

Plural: we, us, you, they, them

Possessive: my, mine, her, hers, his, our, ours, your, yours, their, theirs

Three elements determine which pronoun to use: case, person, and number.

Case: The cases of personal pronouns are nominative, objective, and possessive.

	NOMINATIVE CASE	OBJECTIVE CASE	POSSESSIVE CASE
1st Person	I, we	me, us	my, mine, our, ours
2nd Person	you	you	your, yours
3rd Person	he, she, it, they	him, her them, it	his, her, hers its, their, theirs

When a pronoun is the subject of a sentence, use the **nominative case.**

I write books. (*Not* Me write books.)

When a pronoun is the direct or indirect object, use the **objective case.**

Give me the book.

When a personal pronoun shows possession, use the **possessive case.** Possessive pronouns tell *who* or *what* something belongs to.

> The leather-bound book is <u>mine</u>.

Possessive pronouns can be in front of a noun (*my* toothache, *his* big toe) or stand by themselves (This cell phone is *yours*.)

Person: Person shows who is the speaker, who is spoken to, and who is spoken about. The speaker is the first person (*I, we*). The person spoken to is the second person (*you*). The person or thing spoken about is the third person (*he, she, it, they*).

Number: When the pronoun replaces one person or thing, use a singular pronoun (*I, me, you, she, he, it*). When the pronoun replaces more than one person or thing, use a plural pronoun (*we, you, they, them*).

NOTE: The pronoun *you* is both singular and plural.

Reflexive and intensive pronouns end in *–self* or *–selves* (*myself, themselves, yourself*). **Reflexive pronouns** refer back to someone or something already mentioned.

> *If I'd known I was going to live so long, I'd have taken better care of <u>myself</u>.*—Leon Eldred

Intensive pronouns show emphasis.

> I will drive there <u>myself</u>!

Don't substitute a reflexive pronoun for a personal pronoun.

Wrong: Give the money to Riley and <u>myself</u>.

Right: Give the money to Riley and <u>me</u>.

Relative pronouns connect words. The commonly used relative pronouns are *who, whom, which, that, whoever, whomever, whose,* and *what.*

> Rock journalism is people <u>who</u> can't write interviewing people <u>who</u> can't talk for people <u>who</u> can't read.
> —Frank Zappa

The most common error with relative pronouns is using *who* when it should be *whom* and vice versa. See p. 149.

Demonstrative pronouns are *this, that, these,* and *those.* They point to people or things without actually naming them.

> I'll take six of <u>those</u>.

> I wish I could play the piano like <u>that</u>!

> Marisela didn't buy any property; <u>this</u> is no way to win Monopoly.

> Cross out every sentence until you come to one you cannot do without. <u>That</u> is your beginning.—Gary Provost

When *this, that, these,* and *those* precede a noun, they are adjectives, not pronouns: *that* book, *those* pickles.

Indefinite pronouns, as their name suggests, are rather vague. Examples are *any, all, several, few, some, each, every,* and compounds with *-body, -thing,* and *-one* (such as *no one, everyone, somebody, something, nobody, nothing*).

Whatever you have, spend less.—Samuel Johnson

Those who write clearly have readers; those who write obscurely have commentators.—Albert Camus

Interrogative pronouns ask questions: *who*, *whom*, *which*, *what*, and *whose*.

Politics is the science of who gets what, when, and why.—Sidney Hellman

Isn't it nice that the people who prefer Los Angeles to San Francisco live there?—Herb Caen

Now let's apply the terms discussed here to the art of good writing.

Part Two
The Tools of Writing

I saw a man on a horse with a wooden leg.
See "Avoid Misplaced Modifiers," p. 39.

2 *Grammatical Guidelines*

> It's not just getting the right number of
> words, it's getting them in the right order.
> —John Cleese

For many people, grammar is about as much fun as a poke in the ear with a sharp stick. To them, grammarians are people who focus on nitpicky details just to make life miserable for students.

Actually, grammar helps put our language into a logical, orderly form. It makes subjects agree with verbs, places modifiers where they won't confuse readers (or make them laugh at you), and makes references clear. Communication is smooth when we follow rules. This chapter covers the most important ones.

If you need to brush up on terminology, start with the preceding chapter. If you are comfortable with nouns, verbs, subjects, and predicates, and if you can identify first, second, and third person, just jump right in.

Agreement
Make subject and verb agree both in person and number.

> Agreement is as pleasant in prose as it is in personal relations, and no more difficult to work for.—Jacques Barzun

Errors in agreement are among the most common mistakes writers make. The rule seems simple: A singular subject requires a singular verb; a plural subject requires a plural verb.

Singular:

<u>Tom</u> <u>is</u> late.
sing. sing.
subj. verb

Plural:

<u>Tom and Bill</u> <u>are</u> late.
pl. subj.   pl. verb

A subject in the first person also requires a verb in the first person: *I am* clever.

A subject in the third person requires a verb in the third person: *She is* clever.

But the rule is easier to state than to apply. It's not always clear what the subject is and whether it is singular or plural. So let's look at those two questions: how to identify the subject, and how to determine the number.

How to identify the subject: Three things can complicate your finding the subject.

- Intervening phrases

Phrases that come between subject and verb do not affect the number of the verb.

> <u>Identification</u> of these compounds <u>has</u> remained difficult.
>
> It is my <u>son</u>, not my daughters, who <u>likes</u> to bake bread.
>
> The <u>collision</u> between expanding human demands and Earth's natural limits <u>has</u> created unprecedented challenges.
>
> <u>One</u> in five public water systems <u>contains</u> toxic substances.
>
> *<u>Horse sense</u> is what a horse has that <u>keeps</u> him from betting on people.*—W. C. Fields

Mentally omit words that come between subject and verb to decide whether to use a singular or plural verb.

- Phrases and clauses as subjects

Use a singular verb if the subject is a phrase or clause.

> <u>What this country needs</u> <u>is</u> a good 5-cent nickel.
>   sing. subject   sing. verb
> —F. P. Adams

> <u>The best way to keep your friends</u> <u>is</u> not to give them away.—Wilson Mizner

> <u>The shelf life of the average trade book</u> <u>is</u> somewhere between milk and yogurt.—Calvin Trillin

- Inverted order of subject and verb

When the subject follows the verb, you may have to think twice about whether the verb should be singular or plural.

> Leading the list of Nobel Prize winners <u>was</u> <u>Linus Pauling</u>.
>   sing. verb   sing. subj.

> Seeking to defeat the legislation <u>were</u> <u>half a dozen senators</u>.
>   plural verb   plural subj.

First locate the subject and then you will know what the number of the verb should be (*most* of the time! ☺).

How to determine the number: Watch for five things that determine whether the subject takes a singular or plural verb.

- Compound subjects

Two or more subjects joined by a conjunction (*and, or, nor…*) and having the same verb are a **compound subject.** If the compound subject is joined by *and*, use a plural verb.

The <u>title and abstract</u> of the report <u>appear</u> on the first page.
  compound subj.   plural verb

<u>Writing a report and submitting it for review</u> <u>are</u> difficult tasks for the new manager.

<u>Motherhood and apple pie</u> <u>are endowed</u> with special virtues in the U.S.

If the compound subject is joined by *or, nor, either...or,* or *neither...nor,* make the verb agree with the word just preceding the verb.

Neither the address nor the <u>postmark</u> <u>was</u> legible.
                                 sing.   sing.

Either <u>war</u> <u>is</u> obsolete or <u>men</u> <u>are</u>.—Buckminster Fuller

If you end up with an awkward sentence, rewrite.

Awkward: Neither he nor I am willing to compromise.

Better: He is not willing to compromise; neither am I.

EXCEPTIONS: If a compound subject is regarded as a single unit or refers to the same person or thing, use a singular verb.

Bacon and eggs is a standard breakfast for some people.

My friend and former roommate is coming for a visit.

Compound subjects preceded by *each* or *every* are singular.

Every man, woman, and child is given full consideration.

Each chocolate truffle and pecan cluster is individually wrapped.

Company names, even when they combine several units or names, are usually considered as a single entity and thus take a singular verb.

Hy Skorz & Associates specializes in college testing.

Tanya Hyde & Company manufactures leather goods.

• Collective nouns

Nouns such as *family, couple, group, majority, percent,* and *personnel* take either singular or plural verbs. If the word refers to the group as a whole, or if the idea of oneness predominates, use a singular verb.

The faculty is meeting tonight at seven.

The jury has arrived at its verdict.

The elderly couple was the last to arrive.

A minority may be right; a majority is always wrong.
—Henrik Ibsen

If the word refers to individuals or items within a group, use a plural verb.

The faculty have expressed differing views.

A couple of latecomers were escorted to their seats.

The trouble with the publishing business is that too many people who have half a mind to write a book do so.
—William Targ

In some cases rewriting avoids the problem.

Replace: The jury was clearly moved by the graphic evidence.

with: The jurors were clearly moved by the graphic evidence.

Some words take either singular or plural verbs, depending on how they are used.

Human rights is a sensitive issue. (singular)

Human rights are often ignored. (plural)

Use singular verbs with nouns that are plural in form but singular in meaning, such as *measles*, *checkers*, and *news*.

Measles is a preventable disease.

The news is broadcast daily.

Words ending in *-ics* (*statistics, politics, economics, athletics*) are singular if they refer to a body of knowledge and plural if they refer to particular activities or individual facts.

> <u>Statistics</u> <u>is</u> a difficult subject. (singular)

> The <u>statistics</u> <u>show</u> a declining birth rate. (plural)

> *<u>Politics</u> <u>is</u> perhaps the only profession for which no preparation is thought necessary.*—Robert Louis Stevenson

 The word *number* is singular when preceded by *the* and plural when preceded by *a*.

> The <u>number</u> of students enrolling <u>is</u> decreasing.

> A <u>number</u> of stock market indicators <u>were</u> favorable.

- Indefinite pronouns

The following pronouns are always singular: *another, each, every, either, neither,* and *one,* as are the compound pronouns made with *any, every, some,* and *no* (*anybody, anything, anyone, nobody, nothing, no one…*).

> <u>Neither</u> of the tax returns <u>was</u> completed on time.

> *When it is a question of money, <u>everybody</u> <u>is</u> of the same religion.*—Voltaire

> *An expert is <u>one</u> who <u>knows</u> more and more about less and less.*—Nicholas Murray Butler

> <u>Each</u> of you <u>is</u> welcome to stay.

Nothing is so useless as a general maxim.—Thomas Macaulay

 When the word *each* **follows** a plural subject, it does not affect the verb, which remains plural.

The voters each have their own opinion.

The following pronouns are always plural: *both, few, many, others,* and *several.*

Many are called, but few are chosen.—Matthew 22:14

The following pronouns are either singular or plural, depending on how they are used: *all, none, any, some, more,* and *most.*

We've suffered some setbacks, but all is not lost. (singular)

The mistakes were costly, and all were avoidable. (plural)

None of the laundry was properly cleaned. (singular)

Three people were in the plane, but none were hurt. (plural)

The relative pronouns *who, which,* and *that* are singular if they have singular antecedents (the words they refer to) or plural if they have plural antecedents.

She is one of those rare individuals who follow directions.
                       pl. antecedent   pl. verb

She is the one student who follows directions.
              sing. antecedent   sing. verb

Sometimes rewriting solves the problem and trims wordiness as well.

Replace: Honesty is <u>one</u> of the most important virtues that <u>is</u> discussed in the book.

with: Honesty is one of the most important virtues discussed in the book.

- Expressions of time, money, and quantity

Use a singular verb with a total amount.

Three dollars is a reasonable price.

Use a plural verb when referring to individual units.

Two dollars were enclosed.

- Fractions

The number of the noun following a fraction determines the number of the verb.

Three-fourths of the <u>ballots</u> <u>have</u> been counted.
plural   plural

Three-fourths of the <u>money</u> <u>is</u> missing.
sing. sing.

Democracy is the recurrent suspicion that more than <u>half</u> of the <u>people</u> <u>are</u> right more than half of the time.—E. B. White

Make pronoun and antecedent agree in number.

Agreement is important not only with subjects and verbs, but with pronouns and their antecedents. Both contribute to coherent writing.

The Labour <u>party</u> has nominated <u>its</u> candidate.
    sing. antecedent   sing. pronoun

The Labour and Conservative <u>parties</u> have nominated <u>their</u> candidates.

Each employee provides his or her (*not* their) own tools.

When following this rule means using masculine pronouns for both sexes, some writers choose to ignore the rule. However, you can usually avoid both grammatical error and sexism by rewriting.

Use the second person:

It's enough to drive <u>you</u> out of <u>your</u> senses.

Use a plural noun as antecedent:

The <u>employees</u> provide <u>their</u> own tools.

Parallel Construction

Parallel words, phrases, and clauses improve the flow of ideas and heighten its impact. Similarity of form helps readers recognize similarity of content or function.

We think according to nature; we speak according to rules; we act according to custom.—Francis Bacon

…government of the people, by the people, and for the people.—Abraham Lincoln

Canada has no cultural unity, no linguistic unity, no religious unity, no economic unity. All it has is unity.
—Kenneth Boulding

Express parallel thoughts in grammatically parallel ways. For example, pair a preposition with another preposition, a negative clause with a negative clause, and so on.

In an undeveloped country, don't drink the water; in a developed country, don't breathe the air.—Changing Times

If one person says you're a donkey, don't mind. If two say so, be worried. If three say so, go buy a saddle.
—Yiddish proverb

Sometimes an additional preposition is needed to maintain parallelism.

Wrong: The program is popular in minority communities as well as police officers.

Right: The program is popular in minority communities as well as among police officers.

Use parallel construction in lists, outlines, or headings. If a list begins with strong verbs (a good idea, by the way), make the entire list begin with such verbs. The example below (from a brochure describing a writing course!) switches from strong active verbs to a wordy string of nouns and adjectives.

1. Add impact to every line

2. Explode writing myths

3. The simple techniques used to stimulate readers' interest

Change the third item to something like this:

3. Stimulate readers' interest

Modifiers
Avoid misplaced modifiers.

> Sylvester picked up a girl in a blue jacket named Bonnie.

That's a misplaced modifier. It's everyone's favorite grammatical goof.

> People with deficient metabolizing systems or children may be unjustly burdened by genetically engineered foods.

> One day I decided to look up a style of music I'd been listening to in a big Merriam-Webster dictionary.

> It's a 30-minute documentary on the Bay Area's housing and growth crisis produced by the Association of Bay Area Governments.

I found all those misplaced modifiers in books or magazines, where they had eluded the eye of copyeditors. If you want to avoid having blue jackets named Bonnie in your writing, keep related words together.

Here are some more misplaced modifiers.

> **Wrong:** He told her that he wanted to marry her frequently.
> **Right:** He frequently told her that he wanted to marry her.

> **Wrong:** The clients were told their policy only covers procedures that are medically approved by their insurance agent.
> **Right:** The clients were told by their insurance agent that their policy only covers medically approved procedures.

Wrong: The seminar is designed for adolescents who have been experimenting with drugs and their parents.

Right: The seminar is designed not only for adolescents who have been experimenting with drugs but for their parents as well.

As you can see in the above examples, word order is an indicator of meaning in the English language. Thus, it's important to place modifiers where they convey the intended meaning.

The delightfully descriptive **squinting modifier** seems to refer to words on either side of it.

A plan for laying off workers gradually is getting attention.

What does *gradually* refer to—the plan or the attention? To avoid confusion, place such modifiers directly **preceding** the word or phrase they modify. The intended meaning determines which of the following sentences is correct.

A plan for gradually laying off workers is getting attention.
or
A plan for laying off workers is gradually getting attention.

Avoid dangling modifiers.

A modifier "dangles" when what it modifies is missing or is misplaced in the sentence.

As the author of grammar books, my reputation demands error-free writing.

My reputation is not the author—*I* am!

Jogging across the busy street, a truck almost hit me.

The truck appears to be doing the jogging here. You can repair the sentence in a number of ways.

> Jogging across the busy street, I was almost hit by a truck.

> As I jogged across the busy street, a truck almost hit me.

Subtle danglers may slip by unnoticed.

> After standing in line for half the night, they announced that all the tickets had been sold.

> Having been in the Army, your editorial reminded me of the joys of being a raw recruit.

But some danglers are real howlers for which there's no excuse.

> At the age of five, his father died.

> Hidden in an antique seaman's chest, Aunt Keziah found the crucial document.

> Having been damaged in shipping, I returned the package.

> When dipped in butter, you can experience the lobster's rich flavor.

EXCEPTIONS: Certain modifying phrases are so useful that they are accepted as correct even though they dangle. *All things considered, strictly speaking, judging by the record, curiously, admittedly,* and *assuming you're right* are examples of this well-established idiom.

The word *hopefully* (as in *Hopefully, we will be on time*) should be just as acceptable, but it is still frowned on by some language mavens and by the *New York Times Style Guide*. You can stick with the *Times* or join the crowd of *hopefully* users. You can even skirt the whole issue, as I do, by finding another way to express yourself. (See p. 139.)

Double Negatives
In general, avoid double negatives.

Two negative words tend to cancel each other and create a positive meaning, which may not be what you have in mind.

Wrong: The program is not going nowhere.

Right: The program is going nowhere.

Not all double negatives are so obvious.

Wrong: I couldn't scarcely believe what I heard.

Right: I could scarcely believe what I heard.

Be especially careful when words other than *no* or *not* express negation.

Wrong: The absence of compassion was noticeably lacking.

Right: The lack of compassion was evident.

Note that *neither/nor* does not constitute a double negative; it is more in the spirit of a list of two negative elements.

Neither this nor that...

Avoid complicated negative constructions that burden the reader.

Poor: I couldn't see how it was not a disservice.

Better: I could see that it was a disservice.

You may, however, choose a double negative for its deliberate understatement *(The program is not without merit)*, or for its humorous effect.

If people don't want to come out to the park, nobody's going to stop them.—Yogi Berra

Let's forget it never happened.—Ray Kass

Grammar-Checkers

Though spell-checkers are useful, grammar-checkers are more nuisance than help. Their limited rules fail to catch some mistakes while flagging other parts as errors when they are actually correct.

Altogether, you're better off using *Write Right!* to check your grammar.

𝟛 *Punctuation Pointers*

> *Anyone who can improve a sentence of*
> *mine by the omission or placing of a comma*
> *is looked upon as my dearest friend.*
> —George Moore

Punctuation marks guide your readers. Think of them as language traffic signals: Slow Down, Go That Way, Notice This, Detour. Misleading punctuation can interrupt the flow of ideas and distort meaning, but properly used punctuation helps readers grasp your meaning.

If you find a sentence particularly hard to punctuate, consider rewriting it; the problem may be one of style rather than punctuation. The well-written sentence almost punctuates itself.

Apostrophe '

The apostrophe has moved to the head of my list of misused punctuation marks. Not only is it sometimes omitted where it's needed, but even more often the apostrophe pops up where it doesn't belong (as in *it's conclusion*).

> **Wrong:** Who's chili is tastiest?
> **Right:** Whose chili is tastiest?

Wrong: Tomato's for Sale
Right: Tomatoes for Sale

Wrong: The cell phone is our's.
Right: The cell phone is ours.

Before using an apostrophe, stop to consider whether it fills any of the following needs: to show possession, to show contraction (omission of letters or numbers), or to form plurals of certain letters or words.

Use an apostrophe to show possession in the following cases.

- With singular nouns that don't end in *s*, add *'s*.

writer's cramp	employee's paycheck
witch's brew	nurse's uniform
someone's idea	fox's tail

This rule also applies to proper nouns.

Groucho Marx's mustache

Canada's climate is nine months winter and three months late fall.—Evan Esar

There are two schools of thought about adding *'s* to singular nouns that end in *s*. The traditional approach (Strunk and White, *The Elements of Style*) favors using *'s* at the end of all singular nouns including those ending in *s*.

the boss's decision   the witness's testimony

The modern approach (*N.Y. Public Library Writer's Guide*) is to use the apostrophe only.

the boss' decision   the witness' testimony

I guess that makes me a traditionalist, since *the boss' decision* makes me wonder how to pronounce it, and such a distraction seems undesirable. However, certain expressions ending in *s* (or an *s* sound) traditionally require the apostrophe only.

for goodness' sake   in Moses' lifetime

Rewriting is often the solution for an awkward possessive.

Awkward: Dickens's novels   a friend of mine's car

Better: the novels of Dickens   a friend's car

• With plural words that end in *s*, add only an apostrophe.

teachers' conference	employees' union
the Davises' vacation	witnesses' testimony
nurses' duties	guests' names

Psychiatry enables us to correct our faults by confessing our parents' shortcomings.—Laurence J. Peter

When forming the possessive of a plural noun, be sure to start with the correct plural.

the Joneses' guesthouse

• With plural words that do not end in *s*, add *'s*.

children's hour   women's issues   other people's business

! ! Never use an apostrophe with possessive pronouns (*its*, *hers*, *his*, *theirs*, *yours*, *ours*, *whose*). By definition, these words are already possessive.

The next move is yours (*not* your's).

Wrong: The apostrophe seems to have a life of it's own.
Right: The apostrophe seems to have a life of its own.

Above all, remember that *it's* is a contraction for *it is* or *it has*.

It's easy to put the apostrophe in its place.

• If two or more individuals possess a single item, add 's to the last name only.

Tom and Dick's boat (one boat)

- If two or more individuals possess two or more items, add 's to each noun.

  Tom's and Dick's boats (two boats)

- With singular compound words, add 's to the end of the last word.

  son-in-law's car   notary public's seal
  Master-of-Ceremony's greeting   major domo's baton

- With plural compound words, use a phrase beginning with *of* to show possession.

  Awkward: the attorneys general's meeting

  Better: the meeting of the attorneys general

See p. 118 regarding formation of plural compounds.

- Use ' or 's in established idiomatic phrases even though ownership is not involved.

| two dollars' worth | a month's vacation |
| a stone's throw | today's jittery market |

five years' experience (*or* five years of experience)

Sometimes a hyphenated form is better: *a two-week vacation.*

Use an apostrophe in contractions to indicate omission of letters or numbers.

| summer of '02 | can't | he's |
| they're | you'd | sec'y |

I'm not denyin' the women are foolish: God Almighty made 'em to match the men.—George Eliot

If you think you're too small to make a difference, then you've never spent a night in bed with a mosquito.
—Anita Roddick

Contractions create a friendly, informal tone that may not be suitable in formal writing.

 If you aren't sure about a contraction, mentally reinsert the missing letters to see if it makes sense.

You're welcome to stay here. (You are…)

If, upon doing this, you uncover a grammatical error, rewrite.

Wrong: There's three reasons… (There is three reasons… Oops!)
Right: There are three reasons…

Use an apostrophe to form certain plurals.

- In abbreviations that have periods

  M.D.'s   Ph.D.'s

- With letters when the addition of *s* alone would be confusing

  p's and *q*'s
  The instructor handed out few *A*'s.

- In words used merely as words without regard to their meaning

  Don't give me any *if*'s, *and*'s, or *but*'s.

Avoid using 's in the following cases:

- With titles

  Poor: *All's Well That Ends Well*'s ending
  Better: the ending of *All's Well That Ends Well*

- With abbreviations or acronyms

  Poor: NHL's rulings
  Better: NHL rulings

- With awkward possessives

Use an *of* phrase to avoid an awkward possessive.

  Poor: the Tower of London's interior
       a relative of mine's estate

  Better: the interior of the Tower of London
       the estate of a relative of mine

- With a name or title that is more descriptive than possessive

    Actors Equity   *Publishers Weekly*

But be careful! When I saw the following headline, I wondered how the employees had been "done" in the first place.

    Wrong: Stanford Employees Report Being Redone

    Better: Stanford Employees' Report Being Redone

Colon ⠒

The colon is a mark of anticipation, as the following rules illustrate.

Use a colon in the following cases:

- To introduce a list, summary, long quotation, or final clause that explains or amplifies what precedes the colon

    People have one thing in common: They are all different.
    —Robert Zend

    That money talks, I'll not deny.
    I heard it once: It said "Goodbye."
    —Richard Armour

    When I am dead, I hope it may be said: "His sins were scarlet, but his books were read."—Hillaire Belloc

    In two words: im possible.—Samuel Goldwyn

Capitalize the first letter following the colon only if it begins a complete statement or a quotation. (See p. 96.)

- Following the words *as follows* or *the following*

  The recipe called for the following ingredients: black chanterelle mushrooms, Thai fish sauce, chipotle peppers, and golden caviar.

The concept of "as follows" may be implicit.

  In our country we have three unspeakably precious things: freedom of speech, freedom of conscience, and the prudence never to practice either.—Mark Twain

- In formal salutations

  Dear Senator Blowhard:

- With ratios

  2:1

- To indicate dialogue

  Margaret Fuller: I accept the universe.
  Thomas Carlyle: Gad! She'd better!

- To separate a title and subtitle

  Better Letters: A Handbook of Business and Personal Correspondence

! Do not place a colon immediately after a verb.

Wrong: Prerequisites for the course are: two years of history, Sociology 101, and fluency in Spanish.

Right: Prerequisites for the course are two years of history, Sociology 101, and fluency in Spanish.

Comma 9

In their search for an all-purpose rule, some writers place a comma wherever they would pause or take a breath when speaking. This heavy-breathing school of punctuation may leave readers feeling somewhat winded. On the other hand, too few commas create misunderstandings. You need to chart a course between those extremes, placing commas where they help readers grasp your meaning.

Use a comma to separate independent clauses that are joined by coordinating conjunctions.

An independent clause, also know as the main clause, makes a complete statement; the coordinating conjunctions are *and, but, or, nor, for, yet,* and *so*. (The clauses are underlined in the following examples.)

> The English are not a very spiritual people, so they invented cricket to give them some idea of eternity.
> —George Bernard Shaw

> The writer is not the person, yet both natures are true.
> —Fay Weldon

> The optimist proclaims that we live in the best of all possible worlds, and the pessimist fears this is true.
> —James Branch Cabell

> *Acrobats start their children on the high wire as soon as they can walk, and a writer ought to begin before he has graduated to solid food.*—Robertson Davies

Unless a comma is needed to prevent misreading, you may omit it between short, closely related clauses.

> *Keep your face to the sunshine and you cannot see the shadow.*—Helen Keller

> *I saw the angel in the marble and I just chiseled till I set him free.*—Michelangelo

> *Give a little love to a child and you get a great deal back.* —John Ruskin

> *Any fool can make a rule and every fool will follow it.* —Henry David Thoreau

If the clauses are long and contain commas, separate them with a semicolon rather than a comma.

> *If a man begins with certainties, he shall end in doubts; but if he will be content to begin with doubts, he shall end in certainties.*—Francis Bacon

Use a comma between the dependent and main clauses only when the dependent clause precedes the main clause. (Dependent clauses are incomplete statements; they are underlined in the following examples.)

> *As scarce as truth is, the supply has always been in excess of demand.*—Josh Billings

If you keep your mind sufficiently open, people will throw a lot of rubbish in it.—William A. Orton

If at first you don't succeed, don't take any more chances. —Kin Hubbard

Run-ons and comma faults are common errors. A **run-on,** as its name suggests, is two independent clauses that are not separated by punctuation or a conjunction. To correct the error, provide the separation by adding a period, semicolon, or comma.

Run-on: A good catchword can obscure analysis for 50 years it's the difference between a philosophy and a bumper sticker.
Corrected: A good catchword can obscure analysis for 50 years. It's the difference between a philosophy and a bumper sticker.

Run-on: Teamwork is not a preference it's a necessity.
Corrected: *Teamwork is not a preference, it's a necessity.*
—John Wooden

A **comma fault** is two independent clauses connected only by a comma or by a conjunctive adverb such as *however*. Correct the error by replacing the comma with a semicolon or period.

Comma fault: The trial itself was televised, however, reporters were barred from the courtroom during jury selection.
Corrected: The trial itself was televised; however, reporters were barred from the courtroom during jury selection.

Comma fault: Some sentences are too long, they should be broken up into more manageable chunks.
Corrected: Some sentences are too long. They should be broken up into more manageable chunks.

Use commas to separate three or more items in a series.

peanuts, popcorn, and potato chips

Early to rise and early to bed
Makes a man healthy, wealthy, and dead.
—Ogden Nash

Writing is just having a sheet of paper, a pen, and not
a shadow of an idea of what you're going to say.
—Francoise Sagan

Although journalists tend to omit the final comma to save space, language authorities recommend retaining the final comma to avoid confusion. In the following sentences, you can see the kind of trouble caused by omission of the final comma.

In the tabloids, you can read about alien life forms, the woman who gave birth to 27 babies and Elvis Presley.

The 15-member marching band, a drum major carrying the flag and 20 Girl Guides were all part of the Canada Day parade.

The elements in a series may be short independent clauses.

The only way to keep your health is to eat what you don't want, drink what you don't like, and do what you'd rather not.—Mark Twain

Animals have these advantages over man: They have no theologians to instruct them, their funerals cost them nothing, and no one starts lawsuits over their wills.—Voltaire

Always grab the reader by the throat in the first paragraph, sink your thumbs into his windpipe in the second, and hold him against the wall until the tag line.—Paul O'Neil

First have something to say, second say it, third stop when you have said it, and finally give it an accurate title.—John Shaw Billings

In America only the successful writer is important, in France all writers are important, in England no writer is important, and in Australia you have to explain what a writer is.—Geoffrey Cotterell

When each element in the series is joined by conjunctions such as *and* or *or*, omit the commas.

> *As soon as questions of will or decision or reason or choice of action arise, human science is at a loss.*—Noam Chomsky

Use commas between consecutive adjectives that modify the same noun.

an inexpensive, worthwhile program

Both *inexpensive* and *worthwhile* modify the noun *program*.

> *Conscience is a still, small voice that makes minority reports.*—Franklin P. Jones

> *The muse in charge of fantasy wears good, sensible shoes.*—Lloyd Alexander

When the first adjective modifies not the noun alone but a combination of the second adjective and the noun, omit the comma.

average urban voter	cold roast beef
white tennis shoes	short attention span

Average modifies *urban voter*, not just *voter*; *white* modifies *tennis shoes*, and so on.

 One way to determine whether consecutive adjectives modify the same noun (*a young, energetic student*) is to insert the word *and* between the adjectives. "Young and energetic student" makes sense, but "short and attention span" doesn't. Use a comma between adjectives only if *and* would be a plausible alternative.

The phrase *an ugly, old fur coat* illustrates both where to use a comma and where to omit it. *Ugly and old* sounds right, but *old and fur coat* doesn't; hence, only *ugly* and *old* are separated by a comma.

white tennis shoes   *ugly, old fur coat*

Use commas where needed for clarity.

- To separate identical or similar words

  Whatever you're going to do, do it right.

- To provide a pause or avoid confusion

  Fashion passes, style remains.—Coco Chanel

Most of us would momentarily misread sentences such as the following, from which I removed the commas.

  If he chooses Williams can take over the program.

  Even though I was young when she told me that I understood her meaning.

  There were no frontiers left behind which one could hide.

  As the corpse went past the flies left the restaurant table in a cloud and rushed after it.—George Orwell

- To indicate omission of a word or words

  When angry, count to ten before you speak; if very angry, a hundred.—Thomas Jefferson

Use commas to set off certain elements.

- Contrasting words or phrases

  Advice is judged by results, not by intentions.—Cicero

  The fool wonders, the wise man asks.—Benjamin Disraeli

  The less you write, the better it must be.—Jules Renard

A writer doesn't die of heart failure, but of typographical errors.—Isaac Bashevis Singer

The beautiful part of writing is that you don't have to get it right the first time, unlike, say, a brain surgeon.
—Robert Cormier

My objective is to show what I found, not what I was looking for.—Pablo Picasso

Make everything as simple as possible, but not simpler.
—Albert Einstein

Fiction is not photography, it's oil painting.
—Robertson Davies

- Phrases that are parenthetical, disruptive, or out of order

  Pessimism, when you get used to it, is just as agreeable as optimism.—Arnold Bennett

  Great blunders are often made, like large ropes, of a multitude of fibers.—Victor Hugo

  Every man is, or hopes to be, an idler.—Samuel Johnson

  Books, if you don't put them first, tend to sulk. They retreat into a corner and refuse to work.—Salman Rushdie

- Nonrestrictive phrases (phrases that add nonessential information)

  The greatest discovery of my generation is that human beings, by changing the inner attitudes of their minds, can change the outer aspects of their lives.—William James

To knock a thing down, especially if it is cocked at an arrogant angle, is a deep delight of the blood.—George Santayana

An appositive (an explanatory phrase immediately following the word it explains) is often a nonrestrictive phrase.

My mother, <u>the family historian</u>, found some startling information in the 1890 Census.

I have only one mother, so the appositive *the family historian* is not needed to identify her.

Stuart Keate, former publisher of the *Vancouver Sun*, once wrote that Canada is the vichyssoise of nations—cold, half-French, and difficult to stir.

Omit the commas if the phrase is defining (restrictive). In the following examples, the restrictive phrases are underlined; they define which noted economist, which form of taxation, and so on.

The noted economist <u>Milton Friedman</u> described inflation as the one form of taxation <u>that can be imposed without legislation</u>.

The conservative <u>who resists change</u> is as valuable as the radical <u>who proposes it</u>.—Will and Ariel Durant

- Introductory phrases

Fortunately, there are those among us who have a healthy irreverence toward power, even as they seek it.—Weir Reed

In the long run, it is the sum total of the actions of millions of individuals that constitutes effective group action.—Paul Ehrlich

- Direct address

  Reader, suppose you were an idiot. And suppose you are a member of Congress. But I repeat myself.—Mark Twain

  No, Agnes, a Bordeaux is not a house of ill-repute.
  —George Bain

I recently received a promotional letter from a magazine publisher with the following teaser on the envelope:

Are you always the first to know Jan Venolia?

Actually, I know her rather well, but that's not what was meant. Avoid this kind of goof by putting a comma before the name of the person being addressed.

- Direct quotation

  John Ciardi said, "A dollar saved is a quarter earned."

  When asked to describe Charles DeGaulle, Winston Churchill responded, "He looks like a female llama who has just been startled in her bath."

  "Take some more tea," the March Hare said to Alice, very earnestly. "I've had nothing yet," Alice replied in an offended tone, "so I can't take more." "You mean you can't take less," said the Hatter. "It's very easy to take more than nothing."—Lewis Carroll

But commas are not needed before quoted material such as the following:

Clever sayings abound on the Internet, such as "Artificial intelligence is no match for natural stupidity."

See p. 82 regarding other punctuation marks with quotations.

- Following the words *for example*, *that is*, and *namely*

  The evidence all pointed to one conclusion; namely, that the defendant was innocent.

The abbreviations for these phrases are based on Latin words and should also be followed by commas.

e.g. = *exempli gratia* (for example)

i.e. = *id est* (that is)

viz. = *videlicet* (namely)

  The city council considered a proposal to streamline election procedures (i.e., to allow voting by mail).

- Conjunctive adverbs

Put a comma after adverbs that are functioning as conjunctions if you wish to indicate a pause. Examples of conjunctive adverbs are *however*, *therefore*, *indeed*, *thus*, and *consequently*.

  A shortage of platinum has halted production; consequently, we are unable to fill your order at this time.

! ! The punctuation mark **preceding** the conjunctive adverb should be either a semicolon or a period, not a comma. (See p. 87.)

- Informal salutations

  Dear Tom,

- Dates and numbers

  Your letter of July 4, 1776, answers all my questions.

Put commas both before and after the year when a date is written in month-day-year order. If the date is written in day-month-year order, omit the commas.

  Your letter of 4 July 1776 answers all my questions.

For U.S. style, the use of a comma in a four-digit number is preferred (1,000); British and scientific styles omit the comma (1000). European style separates large numbers (five or more digits) with thin spaces rather than commas.

  European style: 1 426 396   45 204

  U.S. style: 1,426,396   45,204

Do not use commas in the following cases:

- Between subject and verb

  Wrong: Placing a comma between subject and verb, is incorrect.

  Wrong: Riding motorcycles, hang-gliding, and skydiving, were the main pastimes in her short life.

This error frequently occurs when a comma is placed following the last item in a series.

- Between modifier and the word modified, unless what intervenes is parenthetical or nonrestrictive (see p. 62)

  Wrong: a concise, readable, report

  Right: a concise, readable report

  Right: a concise, though readable, report

- Between elements of a compound predicate

  Wrong: On Friday I phoned his office, and was told he was not in.

  Right: On Friday I phoned his office and was told he was not in.

  He sows hurry and reaps indigestion.
  —Robert Louis Stevenson

- Between an independent and a dependent clause when the independent clause comes first (see p. 55)

  You never realize how short a month is until you pay alimony.—John Barrymore

  Everything is funny as long as it is happening to someone else.—Will Rogers

  You must always plant your feet firmly on the ground if you want to be able to jump up in the air.—Joan Miró

Dash ▭

Years ago, all you needed to know about typing a dash was that it consisted of two hyphens, with no spaces before or after it.

Now, with the refinements of desktop publishing, you should know the difference between the four kinds of dash: the em, the en, the 2-em, and the 3-em dash. By choosing the right dash for the job, you produce copy that more closely resembles typeset material.

Use the em dash (two hyphens on a typewriter keyboard) for emphasis, to indicate an abrupt change, or with explanatory words or phrases.

> *It may be that the race is not always to the swift, nor the battle to the strong—but that is the way to bet.*
> —Damon Runyon

> *People want to know why I do this, why I write such gross stuff. I like to tell them I have the heart of a small boy—and I keep it in a jar on my desk.*—Stephen King

Use a pair of em dashes to replace parentheses.

> *Though motherhood is the most important of all the professions—requiring more knowledge than any other department in human affairs—there was no attention given to preparation for this office.*—Elizabeth Cady Stanton

Dashes used in this way may indicate sloppy writing. Can you substitute a comma, colon, or parentheses? Reserve the dash for those instances when you want a sharper break than a comma would provide or a more dramatic aside than you would achieve with parentheses.

> *Unwarranted dashes, the lazy author's when-in-doubt expedient, typify the gushy, immature, breathless style associated with adolescent's diaries.*—Claire Kehrwald Cook

Use the en dash (one hyphen on a typewriter keyboard) between inclusive numbers or dates.

1920–1930

pp. 106–7

! Do not use an en dash following words like *from* or *between*.

Wrong: from 1920–30
Right: from 1920 to 1930

Wrong: The document was written between 1875–1880.
Right: The document was written between 1875 and 1880.

Use the en dash with compound modifiers consisting of two or more words or a hyphenated word.

St. Paul–Minneapolis area

part-Hawaiian–part-Asian ancestry

Use the en dash to join a prefix or suffix to a compound.

> post–World War I

Use the 2-em dash (four hyphens on a typewriter keyboard) to show that part of a word or name has been omitted.

> Ms. S——
> d——n

Use the 3-em dash (six hyphens on a typewriter keyboard) to show that an entire word has been omitted and to avoid repeating an author's name in a bibliography.

> The suspects, —— and ——, were led away shouting.
>
> Venolia, Jan, *Better Letters,* Ten Speed Press, Berkeley, CA, 1995.
> ——, *Kids Write Right!,* Ten Speed Press, Berkeley, CA, 2000.
> ——, *Rewrite Right!,* Ten Speed Press, Berkeley, CA, 2000.

Ellipsis Points o o o

Ellipsis points are three equally spaced periods; they indicate omission of words or the trailing off of a thought at the end of a sentence.

Use ellipsis points to indicate an omission in quoted material.

In the middle of a sentence, use three periods.

> *The salary of the chief executive of a large corporation...is frequently a warm personal gesture by the individual to himself.*—John Kenneth Galbraith

Between sentences, retain the period or other punctuation mark that ends the sentence before the omission.

> *The speaker may be forgiven if he becomes entangled in a hopeless sentence structure, but not so the writer....The speaker can use intonation, facial expression, and gesture to help where his language is lame, but written words lie quietly on the page.*—Theodore Bernstein

Retain punctuation on either side of the ellipsis points if it helps clarify the meaning.

> *Virtually every important domestic change in the United States in recent years has been bottom up. From civil rights to the women's movement to tax revolt,...the public has been the leader and the leadership has been the follower.*
> —Daniel Yankelovich

If entire paragraphs are omitted, retain the end punctuation of the paragraph preceding the omission and add three dots. Additional dots at the beginning of the next paragraph are unnecessary unless words are also omitted from the opening sentence.

Exclamation Point !

The exclamation point is included in this listing of punctuation marks not so much to suggest ways to use it as to caution against overusing it. Since exclamation points add urgency, surprise, or disbelief to a statement, a reader subjected to many of them begins to discredit the emotion and feel somewhat pummeled. Make the words themselves do the work.

The limited usefulness of exclamation points is brought home by the writing instructor who warns her students they will have only three exclamation points to use during their entire lifetime. A book reviewer reveals a similar viewpoint with his comment that "the book bristles with exclamation points." That said, here's where to use them.

Use an exclamation point in the following cases:

- Following an interjection

  Oops!   Congratulations!   Cool!

- Following an exclamatory statement

  I couldn't believe it when I heard the words "and the Oscar goes to…"!

- Following an imperative statement

  Don't do that again!

Place exclamation marks within quotation marks only when they are part of the quotation.

  We were startled to hear someone yell, "Man overboard!"

Hyphen ⊐

Whether to use a hyphen involves some individual choices. One person may write a compound as one word because that's what the dictionary advocates, while another sticks with the hyphenated form because it's easier to read. I tend to fall in the latter category.

I'll give the last word on hyphens to the editors of *Stet Again! More Tricks of the Trade for Publications People*:

> Hyphens exist primarily to avoid ambiguity and speed readers along. ...Everyone agrees it's better to use a hyphen where it's *not* needed than to leave it out where it's essential for sense.

See p. 116 for more discussion of compound words; see p. 97 for capitalization of hyphenated words.

Use a hyphen with certain prefixes:

- With *self-*, *ex-*, and *vice-*

    self-made   ex-wife   vice-chair

- To avoid doubling or tripling a letter

    semi-independent   anti-incumbent
    part-time   shell-like

- If the root word begins with a capital letter

    sub-Saharan   non-Euclidean   pre-Columbian

- To promote clarity

un-ionized	anti-abortion	co-parenting
co-worker	re-read	multi-ply

  Confusing: Recovering the sofa is next on my list of household jobs.
  Clear: Re-covering the sofa is next on my list of household jobs.

Use a hyphen to form certain compound words.

Compound words unite two or more words, with or without a hyphen, to convey a single idea. Wherever possible, write compound words as one word (download, webmaster, turnkey, stockbroker); however, retain the hyphen in the following cases:

- In compound nouns, where needed for clarity or as an aid to pronunciation

right-of-way	editor-in-chief
dot-com	president-elect
come-on	sergeant-at-arms

  Since television, the well-read are being taken over by the well-watched.—Mortimer Adler

- In titles that describe a dual function

secretary-treasurer	soldier-statesman	CEO-Chair

but not job titles that describe a single function.

attorney general	chief executive officer

- With improvised compounds

  know-it-all   stick-in-the-mud

  Johnny-come-lately   ne'er-do-well

  He spoke with a certain what-is-it in his voice, and I could see that if not actually disgruntled, he was far from being gruntled.—P.G. Wodehouse

  The authors adopted an I-can-laugh-at-it-now-but-it-was-no-laughing-matter-at-the-time attitude.—Theodore Bernstein

- With "suspended compounds"

  first-, second-, and third-quarter earnings

- In compound adjectives (unit modifiers) when they precede the word they modify

  off-the-record statement   well-known fact

  user-friendly software   state-of-the-art technology

  cost-of-living increase   London-based company

  It is important to possess a short-term pessimism and a long-term optimism.—Adrienne Rich

If modifiers follow the words they modify, they are no longer compound adjectives, and no hyphens are used.

  The unit is well designed.

  Their accounting methods are up to date.

Idiomatic usage retains the hyphen in certain compounds regardless of the order in which they appear in the sentence.

Tax-exempt bonds can be purchased.

The bonds are tax-exempt.

Be sure to hyphenate all the words that are to be linked.

10-year-old boy, *not* 10-year old boy

 If each of the adjectives could modify the noun without the other adjective, more than a single idea is involved (i.e., it is not a compound adjective), and a hyphen is not used.

a happy, healthy child
a new digital alarm clock

Helpful lists of compound words can be found in the *New York Public Library Writer's Guide*, *The Chicago Manual of Style*, and the *Style Manual* published by the U.S. Government Printing Office. A recent-edition dictionary will provide their editors' views on the status of various compound words (two words, hyphenated, one word). See p. 116 for more about compound words.

Is a misreading or alternative meaning possible when you omit a hyphen? If you mean *re-creation*, for example, you would give readers the wrong idea if you wrote *recreation*. Avoid creating confusing or unintentionally humorous phrases by adding all the necessary hyphens.

Confusing	Clear
caffeine free iced tea	caffeine-free iced tea
toxic waste disposal	toxic-waste disposal
man eating shark	man-eating shark
little used car	little-used car
old film buff	old-film buff
drive by assailant	drive-by assailant
self storage units	self-storage units
30 odd guests	30-odd guests

30 odd guests

Use a hyphen in the following cases:

- In fractions and compound numbers from 21 to 99

  three-fourths   thirty-seven

  Writing is one-third imagination, one-third experience, and one-third observation.—William Faulkner

- To combine numeral-unit adjectives

  12-inch ruler   5-cent cigar
  30-day month   100-year lifespan

- To combine an initial capital letter with a word

  T-shirt   X-rated
  U-turn   V-neck

- To divide a word at the right-hand margin

Do not hyphenate adverbs ending in -ly when combined with an adjective or participle.

Wrong: widely-held stock
          highly-regarded individual

Right: widely held stock
          highly regarded individual

See p. 97 for capitalization of hyphenated words.

Parentheses ( )

Parentheses are dropped into a sentence to enclose less important or explanatory information. They have the effect of an aside, as if you were trying to say the words behind your hand, so they are easily overused.

Use parentheses in the following cases:

- To set off explanatory or nonessential matter

  It is only in good writing that you will find how words are best used, what shades of meaning they can be made to carry, and by what devices (or lack of them) the reader is kept going smoothly or bogged down.—Jacques Barzun

- To provide or spell out an acronym

  Global oil supply is influenced by OPEC (Organization of Petroleum-Exporting Countries).

Punctuate sentences with parentheses as follows:

When the parenthetical matter is a complete statement, enclose punctuation within the parentheses.

  (Don't expect me until nightfall.)

When a parenthetical item falls in the middle or at the end of a sentence, place the necessary punctuation after the closing parenthesis.

  If I arrive late (and it's quite likely), I'll let myself in.

Do not put a comma, semicolon, or dash before an opening parenthesis.

  Wrong: When I arrive, (even if it's late), I'd appreciate a cup of soup.

Right: When I arrive (even if it's late), I'd appreciate a cup of soup.

The New York Public Library Writer's Guide suggests keeping the following distinctions in mind: Parentheses deemphasize information, dashes emphasize information, and commas indicate that the information is simply part of the sentence.

Question Mark ?

Place a question mark at the end of an interrogative sentence.

> *How do I know what I think until I see what I say?*
> —E. M. Forster

> *I love revisions. Where else in life can spilled milk be transformed into ice cream?*—Katherine Paterson

Do not place a question mark at the end of an indirect question or courteous request.

> He asked who would be writing the report.

> Will you please sign all the documents at the space provided.

Quotation Marks " "

Quotation marks are useful for setting off dialogue, quoted material, and special uses of words.

Use quotation marks to indicate a direct quotation.

Oscar Levant said of a politician, "He'll double-cross that bridge when he gets to it."

"I'm world famous," Dr. Parks said, "all over Canada." —Mordecai Richler

Balanchine wanted to get me not to worry about making a masterpiece every time. "Just keep making ballets," he used to say, "and every once in a while one will be a masterpiece."—Jerome Robbins

Do not use quotation marks for an indirect quotation (a restatement of someone's words).

According to Robert Frost, a jury is twelve persons chosen to decide who has the better lawyer.

If a quotation consists of several paragraphs, do one of the following:

- Place a quotation mark at the beginning of each paragraph and at the end of the final paragraph.

- Indent and single-space the text, omitting the quotation marks.

Use single quotation marks to indicate a quote within a quote.

Friedrich Nietzsche said, "He who has a 'why' to live can bear almost any 'how.'"

Kin Hubbard wrote, "When a fellow says, 'It ain't the money but the principle of the thing,' it's the money."

Punctuate quoted material as follows:

- Place the comma and final period inside the quotation marks.

  When asked by an anthropologist what America was called before the white man came, a Native American said simply, "Ours."—Vine Deloria, Jr.

- Place other punctuation marks outside the quotation marks unless they are part of the material being quoted.

  She had the audacity to say "No"!

  You've heard of the three ages of man: youth, middle age, and "You're looking wonderful!"—Cardinal Spellman

  Do you watch "Nova"?

  On being told that President Coolidge had just died, Dorothy Parker asked, "How could they tell?"

Use quotation marks in the following cases:

- To set off individual words or a word or phrase that is being defined

  A mystery is a book the publisher thinks will sell better if it has "mystery" on the cover.—Donald E. Westlake

  The word "ventana" is Spanish for window.

  "Qualifying small businesses" means those with fewer than 250 employees.

  The two most beautiful words in the English language are "Check enclosed."—Dorothy Parker

- To enclose words or phrases following such terms as *entitled, the word(s), the term, marked, designated, classified, named, endorsed,* or *signed*

  The document was signed "John Hancock."

  I always wanted to write a book that ended with the word "mayonnaise."—Richard Brautigan

  A commentary on the times is that the word "honesty" is now preceded by "old-fashioned."—Larry Wolters

  Every word she writes is a lie, including "and" and "the."
  —Mary McCarthy (about Lillian Hellman)

- To indicate a misnomer or special meaning

  Some "antiques" would be more accurately described as junk.

  You may be sure that when a man begins to call himself a "realist," he is preparing to do something he is secretly ashamed of doing.—Sydney Harris

! A word of caution: There's an implicit sneer in this particular use of quotation marks. Don't overdo it. There is also the danger that you might be misunderstood. You'll find an amusing collection in the Gallery of "Misused" Quotation Marks at www.juvalamu.com/qmarks/. A few examples from the Web site:

- A list of ingredients that includes "real" bacon bits (maybe those are for vegetarians?)

- The law firm brochure that claims to maintain "honor and integrity" in the legal profession

- The sign in a market window that reads "Fresh" Fish

Presumably the person putting the quotation marks around a word like "fresh" did not intend to cast doubt on the word, but that's the effect created by this usage.

Unfortunately, new sightings of misused quotation marks are reported to the Web site regularly, so the list grows.

Do not use quotation marks to set off an expression that follows such words as *known as*, *called*, and *so-called* unless the expression is a misnomer or slang.

> *Most of our so-called reasoning consists in finding arguments for going on believing as we already do.*
> —James Harvey Robinson

Use quotation marks to enclose titles of parts of whole publications.

- Chapters or other divisions of a book

- Articles in a periodical

- Stories, essays, poems, and the like, in anthologies or similar collections

See p. 101 for rules regarding italicized titles.

Use quotation marks to enclose titles of songs and television and radio programs.

"Rule, Brittania"

"60 Minutes"

"A Prairie Home Companion"

Semicolon ;

The semicolon provides a stronger break than a comma, a weaker break than a period. It is a useful punctuation mark that careful writers employ to good effect.

> *It is almost always a greater pleasure to come across a semicolon than a period. ...You get a pleasant feeling of expectancy; there is more to come; read on; it will get clearer.*—George R. Will

However, not all writers feel so sanguine toward semicolons.

> *Semicolons are pretentious and overactive.... Far too often, they are used to gloss over an imprecise thought. They place two clauses in some kind of relationship to one another, but relieve the writer of saying exactly what the relationship is.*—Paul Robinson

If you decide that semicolons are a pleasure rather than pretentious, here's how to use them.

Use a semicolon in the following cases:

- Between closely related independent clauses that are not joined by a conjunction

The believer is happy; the doubter is wise.
—Hungarian proverb

Few people think more than two or three times a year; I have made an international reputation for myself by thinking once or twice a week.—George Bernard Shaw

Journalism allows readers to witness history; fiction gives its readers the opportunity to live it.—John Hersey

The semicolon gives equal weight to the clauses it joins, though each needs the other for full meaning.

- To separate long or complicated items in a series

  The lottery winners included an elderly gentleman who had never before bought a lottery ticket; a high school student hoping to use the winnings for college; and a reporter who had bought her ticket while covering corruption in the lottery system.

- Between independent clauses that are long or contain commas

  A neurotic is the man who builds a castle in the air; a psychotic is the man who lives in it; and a psychiatrist is the man who collects the rent.—Lord Webb-Johnson

- Between explanatory phrases that are introduced by such words as *for example*, *that is*, or *namely*

  The students are preparing sophisticated entries for next week's Science Fair; for example, one electronics whiz is building a virtual-reality robot.

- To separate independent clauses when they are linked by such conjunctive adverbs as *however, thus, accordingly, indeed,* and *therefore*

PROJECTIONS WERE GLOOMY

HOWEVER, SALES SKYROCKETED.

Wrong: The coach will be late for the award ceremony, however, he does plan to attend.

Right: The coach will be late for the award ceremony; however, he does plan to attend.

Slash /

The slash is also known as the virgule, diagonal, and slant. Although it appears in informal writing more frequently now than when *Write Right!* was first published, it has limited use in formal writing.

Use the slash as a stand-in for a word or words.

- For the word *to*

  price/earnings ratio

- For the word *per*

  100 miles/hour

- For the word *or*

  and/or   his/her

- For the word *and*

  the July/August issue

- To shorten a popular expression

  24/7 (24 hours a day, 7 days a week)

However, not all of these uses of the slash can be justified. *And/or* smacks of legalese and may leave readers puzzled as to whether the slash replaces *and* or *or*. End the confusion by using one or the other. I find *he/she* hard to read, and *s/he* even more so. To avoid gender bias, use the alternatives suggested on page 37.

Occasionally, the slash indicates that the writer didn't take the time to think clearly and just cobbled together a couple of words for the reader to sort out. If a slash represents sloppy writing, rewrite.

Poor: The actress met with me to promote her movie and to dispel/explain her tumultuous offscreen image.

Better: The actress met with me to promote her movie and to dispel some of the myths behind her offscreen image.

My favorite commentary on the slash was written by Don Hauptman; it first appeared in the *New York Times* and has been widely reprinted.

Gender/Gap

The neutral pronoun "he (slash) she"
    has come into its glory.
In conversations, though, some say,
    it tends to sound quite gory.

The British, in their wisdom, call
    the "/" an oblique stroke,
Which offers a solution for
    the language as it's spoke.

To dodge offensive references
    say "he (oblique stroke) she,"
So no one claims that you endorse
    such gross misogyny.

For surely here's a case in which
    we each react uniquely.
Faced with a choice, would you opt to
    be slashed—or stroked obliquely?

Whether you call it oblique stroke or slash, I still don't like *he/she*.

4 Copyediting Considerations

> *If you get the form of things right,*
> *every peril can be tamed.*
> —Dick Francis

Publishers and large companies often have an in-house style guide to insure uniform handling of such matters as abbreviations, capitalization, and treatment of numbers. But if you're on your own, the following guidelines will help.

When acceptable usage is a matter of personal preference, consistency is the primary consideration. Make a style sheet to keep track of which words you've capitalized, how you treated numbers or compound words, and so on (see illustration on p. 92). Refer to it when you encounter a copyediting choice to see how you handled it previously. Consistency in these matters helps readers concentrate on the subject matter.

STYLE SHEET

A B C D

dialogue	53
bi-lingual	106
bodacious	12
Breathalyzer	46
ad hominem	73

E F G H

Federalism	72, 79
eminence grise	51
halftone	43
freelance	103-5, 110
European Common Market	79

I J K L M

middle-class junkies	66
machismo	67
lowercase	21, 23, 85

N O P Q

question-begging generalization	25
the Pentagon	89
Op-Ed page	66
palimony	67, 69

R S T U V

under way	153
renege	94
right-to-die movement	123
uppercase	21, 23, 86

W X Y Z

white-collar crime	15
win-win situation	12
X-rated films	34

NUMBERS

the 20's	12

ACRONYMS, ABBREVIATIONS

OPEC	34-7
IRA	59

Abbreviations

The term *abbreviation* loosely covers three different condensed forms. An **acronym** is formed from first letters or parts of words and is pronounced as a word (NASA, OPEC). An **initialism** consists of the first letters of words and is pronounced letter by letter (SUV, NGO). An **abbreviation** is a shortened version of a word or phrase (Dept., Sec'y.).

Abbreviations take up less space and speed readers along—if they are in familiar territory. However, what is suitable for one audience may be inappropriate for another. Be aware of how much to expect of your readers. For example, the word *versus* is abbreviated as *v.* in legal citations, as *vs.* in headlines, and written out in text.

A few shortened forms have become words, their origins as acronyms all but forgotten (laser, modem, radar). Some words always appear in abbreviated form (COD, Mr., A.D., p.m.). Unless the shortened form is widely known, however, use the full name the first time it appears, followed in parentheses by the acronym or abbreviation you will use thereafter.

Choosing the correct article (*a* or *an*) to precede an acronym or initialism is important. Acronyms follow the usual rule for consonants and vowels: *a* precedes a consonant (a LAN user), *an* precedes a vowel (an OPEC meeting). But with initialisms, how the initial letter is pronounced determines which article to use. Certain consonants (F, H, L, M, N, R, S, and X) sound as if they begin with a vowel (*f* is pronounced "ef," *r* is "ahr," and so on). If an initialism begins with one of these consonants, *an* is the correct article (an SUV, an NGO).

Abbreviate addresses as follows:

- In an outside address (the address on the envelope), use the postal abbreviation of two capital letters and no period for a state or province. For example, write New York as NY (not N.Y.) and Quebec as PQ.

- Do not abbreviate streets or states in the inside address (the address typed on the first page of a letter). Although this rule is often ignored, observing it gives letters a more elegant appearance.

- Abbreviate compass points that follow street names.

  Porter Street NW   *or*   Porter Street, NW

- Spell out compass points that precede street names.

  1500 South H Street
  One North Broadway

Abbreviate social titles.

Ms. is now an accepted title, comparable to *Mr.* Use *Ms.* in both business and social contexts unless you know that an individual prefers *Miss* or *Mrs.*

The formal plural of the abbreviation *Mr.* is *Messrs.* and of *Mrs.* is *Mmes.* Abbreviate other titles only with the person's full name.

Gen. George S. Patton
Rev. Thomas Carlyle
Gov. Peter Stuyvesant

If the full name is not used, do not abbreviate the title

General Patton, *not* Gen. Patton

In general, abbreviate dates only in informal writing.

Feb. 14, 2010   14 Feb. 2010

With partial dates and in formal usage, write dates in full.

February 14, *not* Feb. 14
14 February, *not* 14 Feb.

Use 's to form the plural of an abbreviation that has periods.

Seventy-three M.D.'s attended the meeting.

Abbreviate the following:

- *United States* and *United Kingdom* only when used as adjectives

U.S. ambassador   U.K. foreign policy

Write out *United States* or *United Kingdom* when used as nouns.

The United States was represented by Vice President Martinez.

The United Kingdom has resisted converting to Eurodollars.

- The word *figure* only in a caption or parenthetical reference

(fig. 1)

Capitalization

Some people have the lazy habit of writing with all capital letters. But text written entirely in capitals is hard to read. Your job is to make the reader's job easier, not harder. What's more, emphasis is lost when everything is emphasized. Which of the following gets the idea across better?

I SAID NO!   *or*   I said NO!

The following rules will help you decide when to use capital letters.

Capitalize the first word of a sentence.

Humor is the shortest distance between two people.
—Victor Borge

The only exception to this rule is when the first word is a proper noun that begins with a lowercase letter (dePriest, von Braun, eNet). If possible, rewrite so that the problem noun no longer begins the sentence.

Capitalize the first word of a complete sentence following a colon.

The company has a new policy: Every employee has three weeks of paid vacation.

Caution: Radioactive material

Do not capitalize the word following a colon if it begins an incomplete statement.

The company has a new policy: three weeks of paid vacation.

Capitalize titles as follows:

- In titles of books, plays, television programs, and so on, capitalize the first and last words, plus all principal words. Do not capitalize articles or conjunctions. Capitalize prepositions if they consist of four or more letters, or if they are connected with a preceding verb.

  Stop the World, I Want to Get Off
  Customers Held Up by Gunmen
  Situation Calls for Action
  Peace Through Negotiation

- Capitalize both parts of a hyphenated word in a title or headline unless it is considered as one word or is a compound numeral.

  Well-Known Actor Dies
  Anti-inflation Measures Taken
  Report of the Ninety-fifth Congressional District
  Son-in-law's Plea

- Capitalize personal titles only if they precede the name and are not separated by a comma.

  Professor Reynolds
  the treasurer, Will Peterson
  Prime Minister Montgomery

Capitalize the following:

- Both full and shortened names of government agencies, bureaus, departments, or services

California Dept. of Corporations *or* Dept. of Corporations
Bureau of Pension Advocates
U.S. Treasury Department, or Treasury Department
Library of Congress
Law Reform Commission
Board of Supervisors
Home Office
Justice Department

Do not capitalize such words as *government*, *federal*, and *administration* except when part of the title of a specific entity.

The U.S. Government is the largest employer in the nation.

She hopes to work for the federal government.

- Points of the compass and regional terms when they refer to specific sections or when they are part of a precise descriptive title

the East	Eastern Europe
the Southern Hemisphere	Vancouver's West End
Mid-Atlantic states	North Pole
the Orient	the Outback
Asia	the Left Bank

Do not capitalize these terms when they are suggesting direction or position.

central states	western provinces	south of town
northern lights	eastern Australia	coastal districts

Go west, young man.—John B.L. Soule

- Proper names but not descriptive words preceding them

  city of Toronto, *not* City of Toronto
  state of Vermont, *not* State of Vermont

- Abbreviations if the words they stand for are capitalized

  M.D.   Ph.D.   M.P.   J.D.   Jr.   a.m.   p.m.

- Ethnic groups, factions, alliances, and political parties but not the word *party* unless it is part of the name

  The Green Party is growing worldwide.

  The Democratic party will be the first to hold its convention.

  He spoke for the Korean community.

Use lowercase for political groupings other than parties.

  She represents the centrist faction of the Newspaper Guild.

  the left wing   the right wing   *but*
  the Left   the Radical Right

Capitalize *African American*, *Caucasian*, *Hispanic*, and *Native American*, but not *blacks*, *whites*, and slang words for the races.

> *With white writers there are a lot of gray areas. There are commercial writers, literary writers, genre writers. But if it's black and it holds a pencil—that's the category.*
> —Wanda Coleman

Problems connected with designation of the races extend beyond questions of capitalization, however. Should you use *Native American* or *American Indian*, *African American* or *black*? Styles in ethnic terminology come and go, and not everyone agrees on any given term. Your best bet is probably to choose the term used by prominent individuals in the particular group.

- Captions and legends according to individual preference or in-house style

  Please refer to figure 5.

  The chart below shows wages by skill level (fig. 5).

In general, use lowercase for the words *figure*, *table*, and *plate* and their abbreviations when they appear in text. Capitalize these terms when they appear in captions.

  Fig. 5—Wages by Skill Level

Do not capitalize the seasons.

  We always look forward to the fall colors.

Italics

Having italic type is one of the joys of word processors. When used correctly, italics enhance the appearance of any document. If you don't have italic type, use underlining.

Use italic type in the following cases:

- Titles of whole works, such as books, magazines, newspapers, movies, plays, and reports

Granta	*Romeo and Juliet*
Washington Post	*Gone with the Wind*
The Hite Report	*Harry Potter and the Sorcerer's Stone*

Do not italicize the word *the* in the name of a newspaper unless it is part of the name.

  Does the library subscribe to the *Washington Post* or *The Cleveland Plain Dealer*?

Use roman type and quotation marks for titles of articles, chapters, poems, essays, and similar short works.

  "Trees"

  "Self-Reliance," by Ralph Waldo Emerson

  Chapter 12, "The Human Use of Human Beings"

- Foreign words unless they are so widely used as to have become familiar

  Black tie is *de rigeur* for the banquet.

  The plane was en route to Algiers when they heard the news.

- For emphasis—occasionally

  Woman was God's *second* mistake.—Friedrich Nietzsche

  The correct detail is rarely exactly what happened; the most truthful detail is what *could* have happened, or what *should* have.—John Irving

  Each time I *agree* with myself, I write an essay. When I *disagree* with myself, I know that I'm pregnant with a short story or a novel.—Amos Oz

- To avoid confusion in cases where words are referred to as words, numbers as numbers, and letters as letters

  The word *alright* should be written as two words, *all right*.

  He wondered why the word *tongue* is feminine in so many languages.

  The *A's* should move to the front of the row, the *B's* next, and so on.

  If the word *arse* is read in a sentence, no matter how beautiful the sentence, the reader will react only to that word. —Jules Renard

- Short quotations when they stand alone, as at the beginning of a chapter

  When you get to the end of your life, be sure you're used up.—Edward Hoagland

Use roman type and quotation marks when the quotation is incorporated into text. (See p. 81.)

> As Mark Twain once said, "Put all your eggs in one basket—and watch that basket."

❗❗ Never use both quotation marks and italics for the same material.

- Punctuation marks that immediately follow an italicized word if they are part of the italicized expression.

> *Write Right!* is a handy reference.

Numbers

When should you write numbers as words and when as figures? That depends on the nature of your writing. Nonetheless, certain conventions about numbers apply in all situations. Observe them to give your writing a professional polish.

Write numbers as words in the following cases:

- From 1 to 9 (in journalism, science, or business); from 1 to 99 (for literary writing)

> *There's an old cowboy's trick. The herd is coming through fast and one cowboy asks another how you estimate the number of cows so quickly. The other cowboy says: "It's very*

easy. You just count the number of hooves and divide by four."—David Mamet

All you need is fifty lucky breaks.—Walter Matthau

- At the beginning of a sentence

  Three hours a day will produce as much as a man ought to write.—Anthony Trollope

  Thirty percent of Americans may write poetry, but I doubt that thirty percent read poetry, even their own.
  —David Lehman

- In round numbers or decades

  several thousand people
  between two and three hundred employees
  in her eighties   the Roaring Twenties

- In fractions standing alone or followed by *of a* or *of an*

  one-fourth inch   two-thirds of a cup
  two one-hundredths   one-half of an apple

  I always try to write on the principle of the iceberg. There are seven-eighths of it under water for every part that shows.—Ernest Hemingway

- To clarify back-to-back modifiers

  three 8-foot planks   six $1/2$-inch strips

Write numbers as figures in the following cases:

- For 10 and above (journalism, science, business); 100 and above (literary writing)

  My efforts to cut out 50,000 words may sometimes result in my adding 75,000.—Thomas Wolfe

- When numbers both below and above 10 refer to the same general subject

  5 of 20 employees
  from 6th to 12th grade

- When they refer to parts of a book

Chapter 9	Figure 5
page 75	Table 1

- With dates and times

  21st century   10 p.m.   5-year plan   January 1, 2010

- When they precede units of time, measurement, or money

18 years old	9 o'clock *or* 9:00
$1.50	75p
2 x 4 inches	$4 million
¼-inch pipe	10 yards
3 hours 30 minutes 12 seconds	

NOTE: Units of time, measurement, and money do not affect the rule determining use of figures when numbers appear elsewhere in the sentence.

Wrong: The 3 students each collected $50.

Right: The three students each collected $50.

Spelling

> *It is a pity that Chaucer, who had geneyus,*
> *was so unedicated. He's the wuss speller*
> *I know of.*—Artemus Ward

Unless you're a humorist like Artemus Ward, misspelling is not an asset. Misspelled words can mislead or confuse readers. They reflect poorly on you as a writer, suggesting carelessness elsewhere.

Spell-checkers help, but they aren't the whole solution. They don't pick up wrong words, particularly homophones *(there, their, they're)*, so they are no substitute for knowing how to spell.

If you consider yourself a bad speller, take a look at one of the books on spelling listed in the bibliography. By learning a few rules (forming plurals, adding suffixes) and by memorizing a few spelling demons (*ei* and *ie* words), you can graduate from the ranks of bad spellers. Use the list of frequently misspelled words that begins on p. 173 as part of a spelling self-help program.

The most enjoyable way to improve spelling is to read good books. Notice how words look. You will absorb correct spellings indirectly, as if through your pores.

The person writing the copy for this ad
should have made use of the dictionary!

Part Three
The Craft of Writing

5 Words

This chapter is about "rooting around," about finding the words you want. Ours is a living language. Anthony Hughes in *The Online English Grammar* urges us to "think of it as a writhing, many-headed, sensual, changing, and wonderful creature."

Some use that vitality to justify accepting all change. If it's what people are doing, they say, it must be right. Paul Lovinger expresses a more reasonable view in *The Penguin Dictionary of American English Usage and Style*:

> New words continually appear. Those that fill needs are generally desirable. What ought to be questioned or resisted are the watering down of distinctive words that we already have, the creation of ambiguity and fuzziness, the breakdown of grace and grammar, and irrational verbal fads.

Admittedly, some changes are useful. New words have been created (*biodiversity, morph, fax, e-mail*) and old words given new meanings (*Web site, hacker, spin*). Rules are reevaluated, and those that serve no purpose disappear. The prohibitions against ending a sentence with a preposition or starting one with a conjunction are good examples.

But when changes "water down" the richness of our language, I resist them. If *nauseous* becomes synonymous with *nauseated*, I begin to feel a little green around the gills. When the noun *loan* crowds out the verb *lend*, we all go into debt. If I've been bitten by a black widow, I need an *antidote*, not someone telling me an amusing story (*anecdote*).

As television gobbles up increasing chunks of the day, the auditory act of hearing replaces the visual act of reading. Along the way, nuances between words disappear, and our writing becomes peppered with malapropisms:

Wrong	Right
for all intensive purposes	to all intents and purposes
one in the same	one and the same
tongue and cheek	tongue in cheek
straightened arrow	straight and narrow

If we allow our language to be whittled down, we lose cultural information; this, in turn, reduces our ability to understand the world and our place in it. Let's use words as our vote for clarity, for felicity, for celebration.

The Prerequisite for Good Writing: A Good Dictionary

A good dictionary is essential in searching for the right word. Among other things, you'll find an exploration of the shades of meaning that will guide your choice.

Take the words *doubtless* and *no doubt*, which my dictionary describes as follows:

> …relatively weak in expressing certainty, since they can also indicate mere presumption or probability: "He will doubtless go"; or concession: "You are no doubt right in some details." In contrast, *undoubtedly* and *without doubt* express only certainty and conviction.

The dictionary goes on to say that *doubt* and *doubtful* are often followed by clauses beginning with *that*, *whether*, or *if*, and it recommends that I look up *doubtful*, *dubious*, and *questionable* for additional shades of meaning. Have I left any doubts that you'll find a dictionary invaluable?

 What *is* a good dictionary? If you're shopping for one, I recommend looking up a few words. If the candidate dictionary lists *heighth* without advising you that this is non-standard usage or if it lists *irregardless* without pointing out the redundancy and suggesting that you use *regardless*, keep looking.

Here are a few of the types of information included in a dictionary:

- Usage, including levels of formality (formal, standard, slang)

- Etymology (word roots)

- Abbreviations

- Pronunciation

- Inflected forms (e.g., *well, better, best*)

- Parts of speech

- Synonyms

A thesaurus, with its everything-under-the-sun approach, expands your choice of alternative wording still further. When Dr. Roget published his first thesaurus in 1852, he said it was for "those who are...struggling with the difficulties of composition." Roget and those who followed have provided us strugglers with an abundance of words to choose from.

As an example, let's walk through the treatment of the word *walk*. It is one of the forty-three categories of entries under "Travel" in my thesaurus. A few of the alternatives included are the highbrow *ambulate*, the descriptive *stride*, the casual *hoof it*, and the quaint *ride shank's mare*. What a treasure trove of choices!

A word processor's dictionary and thesaurus are no substitute for the real thing. When I was considering the wording of the previous paragraph, I looked up *trove* in my word processor's thesaurus. The only alternative it suggested was *trowel*!

A dictionary is helpful *only if you use it.* Look up words often, and while you're there, take advantage of the wealth of information at your fingertips.

> Develop a respect for words and a curiosity
> about their shades of meaning that is almost
> obsessive.—William Zinsser

A Note About British and American Usage

The differences between British English and American English are beyond the scope of this book. Each has a distinct vocabulary, spelling, punctuation, and usage.

American	British
color, jewelry	colour, jewellery
trunk, elevator	boot, lift
Mr.	Mr
in the hospital	in hospital

Nonetheless, our common heritage in language is so extensive that the rules and conventions of American English presented here cover most situations. If you need more information about the differences between British and American English, look at some of the books listed in the bibliography or search the Internet (my search for "British language usage" produced more than 30,000 hits!).

> The Americans are identical to the British in
> all respects except, of course, language.
> —Oscar Wilde

Compound Words

The word *compound* means "consisting of two or more elements." Compound words unite two or more words to convey a single idea. Whether to write compounds as two words (*real estate*), hyphenated (*off-the-record*), or one word (*motherboard*) is a vexed question. Fixed rules are hard to come by.

For example, you can't make a single, all-purpose rule about compounds beginning with the word *cross* since they fall in all three categories: *crossfire*, *cross-country*, and *cross hair*. Let your choice be guided by whether hyphenating a compound helps the reader.

Here are a few suggestions, from the firm to the flexible, for dealing with the compound predicament.

Two-Word Compounds

Some two-word compound nouns go together so naturally that we don't need to add hyphens or make them one word for the sake of clarity. Even when such compounds are modifiers, no hyphens are needed.

Noun	Adjective
civil rights	civil rights attorney
high school	high school graduate
data processing	data processing center

One-Word Compounds

Similarly, some compounds are so well established as one word that we hardly realize they are compounds.

blackout	pickup	wallpaper
checkbook	guidelines	desktop

Others are still evolving toward the one-word form. *Multitasking* has made the transition, while *Web site* is still in the process (*Web site, web site,* and *website* are all currently acceptable). Once you've made a decision, stick with it. If you begin with *start-up companies,* don't switch to *startup companies* mid-document.

Some one-word compounds are formed from a verb and a preposition.

<u>shut</u> + <u>down</u> = shutdown
 verb   prep.

These are handy as nouns (*backup, runoff*) and as modifiers (*a backup procedure, runoff elections*). But you run into trouble if you use such compounds as verbs.

Wrong: Did you backup your file?

Right: Did you back up your file?

By retaining a two-word, unhyphenated verb form such as *back up, run off,* and *set up,* you will avoid a monstrosity like *I back-upped my files.*

Hyphenated Compounds

By hyphenating compound modifiers that precede the noun, you help readers see how the words are connected.

pale-green soup
teacher-training program
part-time employee

See p. 74 for more about hyphenated compounds.

Plural Compound Words

Form plurals of compound words with the principal word.

notaries public   mothers-in-law
attorneys general   major generals
deputy chiefs of staff   commanders in chief
passersby   courts-martial

Medium-size or Medium-sized Business?

The language submits to no rules when it comes to this kind of decision. Certain *-ed* forms are well established.

left-handed pitcher   four-legged animal
two-pronged approach   long-stemmed glasses

But is it *bite-size pieces* or *bite-sized pieces*, *horn-rim glasses* or *horn-rimmed glasses*, *teenage boy* or *teenaged boy*? In *The Careful Writer*, Bernstein concludes that it's a matter of "idiom and sound." In other words, use the form that sounds right to you.

> You can scrutinize whole categories of words and sometimes imagine you have hit upon a principle, but as soon as you do, the next word you can think of constitutes an exception.—Theodore Bernstein

Trendy Words and Clichés

> *Ready-made phrases are the prefabricated strips of words...that come crowding in when you do not want to take the trouble to think through what you are saying.*
> —George Orwell

The saturation provided by television, radio, and the various print media can turn words into instant clichés. *Paradigm, viable options, closure, epiphany, no problem, déjà vu, bottom line, 24/7, basically, radar screen, behind the curve, killer app,* and *rocket scientist* have all joined the catalog of overworked words. A *good news/bad news* format may have been fresh once, but it has lost its edge.

The best way to stifle word fads is to ignore them. Allow the overworked expression to recuperate.

> *My inclination is to question deviant forms, challenge innovations to prove themselves, and resist senseless fads.*—Paul Lovinger

As for clichés, that's where the rubber hits the road. If you're trying to hit the nail on the head and not mince words, it goes without saying that clichés won't do the trick. They seldom throw any light on the subject and probably should never see the light of day. Are we all on the same page?

Jargon

Jargon can be useful shorthand; specialized vocabularies allow members of a professional group to communicate succinctly with each other. But jargon has earned its bad reputation because it is often used simply to impress, or worse yet, to provide a smokescreen for burying truth rather than revealing it. Examples: "revenue enhancement" for taxes and "proactive resource-allocation restructuring" for closing the factory and moving to Mexico.

Everyday jargon includes the following elements: interchangeable parts of speech and noun chains.

Interchangeable Parts of Speech

The English language is remarkably adaptable. It allows us to shuffle parts of speech around, turning nouns into adjectives (*milk carton*), verbs into nouns (*on the mend*), nouns into verbs (*to face*), and adjectives into nouns (*seeing red*). Indeed, such flexibility is one of the strengths of our language. But avoid such "verbs" as *to guest* and *to gift*.

> **Poor:** This model obsoletes its predecessor.
> **Better:** This model makes its predecessors obsolete.

Occasionally pressing nouns into service as verbs (or vice versa) creates a breezy style. In striving for a certain effect, I might write "Let's front-page that story." I would draw the line, however, at "I plan to Op-Ed my views in the Sunday paper" or "The investigator accessed the information in the public library." And I would quickly put aside a handbook on writing if I found a chapter titled "How to Style Written English."

Noun Chains

Nouns used as adjectives often slip out of a writer's control, producing impenetrable chains. To break these into manageable chunks, look for the noun at the end of the chain. Move it forward and turn the other chunks into short prepositional phrases.

> **Rewrite:** potassium permanganate-impregnated activated alumina medium
> **as:** a medium of activated alumina that has been impregnated with potassium permanganate

> **Rewrite:** urban public hospital out-patient clinics
> **as:** out-patient clinics sponsored by urban public hospitals

Revisions of noun chains are often longer than the original phrase. That's a price we pay for clarity. In a contest between brevity and clarity, clarity should always win.

Unintended Meanings and Other Foolishness

Pause to think about what you've written. In the heat of creation, you may fail to notice something as ridiculous as "the world's largest van for its size." Or how about a "precise estimate"? Perhaps you likened a frenzy of activity to the "eye of the storm," when in reality calm is what characterizes the eye of a storm. If you describe a point of new beginning as "ground zero," you are actually referring to the point of maximum impact (hence, maximum destruction), not to fresh ground.

> *The slovenliness of our language makes it easier for us to have foolish thoughts.*
> —George Orwell

Step back and take a fresh look to save yourself embarrassment. Those who wrote the following sentences (all of which appeared in print) failed to do that.

No job losses are planned.

Submit a list of all employees broken down by sex.

No detail is too small to overlook.

We feel pornography is an issue that demands a second look.

Dr. Ruth will talk about sex with Larry King.

(Sign in cemetery) Persons are prohibited from picking flowers from any but their own graves.

Some English words (called **homographs**) have identical spellings but different pronunciations and meanings. Take the word *subject*. When the word is a noun, the accent is on the first syllable (*súbject*) and it means a topic or an individual; when it's a verb, the second syllable is accented (*subjéct*) and it means to cause to undergo.

We had to subject the subject to a series of tests.

Be aware when using a homograph that readers may not know how to interpret a word unless the context makes it clear.

Confusing: The bandage was wound around the wound.

Better: The bandage was tightly wound around the wound.

Better yet: The wound was tightly bandaged.

Tricky Words

English is riddled not only with homographs, but also with homonyms and homophones. **Homonyms** are words that are both spelled and pronounced alike: *bear* the animal and *bear* the verb. **Homophones** are words that have different spellings but the same pronunciation: *write* and *right*. Some words have similar sounds (*home/hone*), and others call for a specific usage (*myriad details*, not *a myriad of details*). No wonder we have trouble!

The following words seem to invite error. Skim through the list to see if it includes words you use and if you're using them correctly. Refer to the list as needed to help you find just the right word and its correct use.

The status of some entries listed below is changing from unacceptable to widely accepted in formal writing. During the transition, careful writers will continue to observe the traditional usage.

Advice, Advise: The noun *advice* means a suggestion or opinion concerning a course of action. The verb *advise* means to give advice; using *advise* as a synonym for *inform* smacks of business jargon. Someone who dispenses advice is either an *adviser* or an *advisor*; both spellings are acceptable, but *adviser* seems to have the edge.

Affect, Effect: *Affect* is most often used as a verb and *effect* as a noun. The verb *affect* means to influence or to have an effect on.

The attorney hopes to affect the jury's decision.

A less common meaning of *affect* as a verb is to pretend in order to make a desired impression.

The prosecutor affected a look of amazement when the defendant couldn't recall his whereabouts.

The noun *effect* means result or consequence.

The effect of the program change was to reduce overtime.

The verb *effect* means to bring about.

Management hopes to effect a similar change in employee benefits.

Aggravate: A verb meaning to make worse. A trouble or condition is aggravated, not a person.

The condition of the road was aggravated by the flooding creek. Esmeralda was provoked (*or* annoyed *or* irritated) when she couldn't reach her mailbox to see if she had won the sweepstakes.

All- (all right, almost, already, altogether): Three of these have both one- and two-word forms, each with its own spelling and meaning. One, *all right,* is correct only in the two-word form; *alright* is a misspelling of *all right.*

The literal meaning of *all right* is entirely right, and its less formal meanings are adequate, permissible, and satisfactory. *Almost* means not quite. *Already* means by this (or a specified) time. *Altogether* means entirely or on the whole.

The two-word forms of these words have different meanings, which you can deduce from the following examples. Failure to note the differences could be embarrassing, as the first example illustrates.

> The cookies and pies are almost baked; you are all most welcome to join us for dinner.

> By the time we were all ready, the plane was already taxiing to the runway.

> They were not altogether happy at being all together again.

Allude, Elude, Refer: To *allude* to something is to mention it indirectly, without identifying it specifically. To *refer* is to indicate directly.

> The speaker alluded to the hazards of smoking when he referred to the chart showing the incidence of lung cancer.

Elude means to slip away from or avoid.

> The suspect managed to elude the police.

Alternate, Alternative: The strict meaning of *alternate* as an adjective refers to every other one, or succeeding by turns: *alternate* days means every other day. It is now more loosely used to mean offering a substitute *(an alternate route).* As a

Alternate

Alternative

noun, *alternate* means a substitute (*an alternate at the convention*). *Alternative* as a noun means a choice (*an alternative to war*). As an adjective, *alternative* has strayed from its strict meaning of one of two choices to mean simply providing a choice (*an alternative plan*).

Ante-, Anti-: *Ante* means coming before or in front of.

antebellum   =   before the war
antediluvian =   before the floods

Anti means against.

antifreeze   anti-establishment

Just to confuse matters, *anti* is also a variant of *ante* in such words as *antipasto*, where it means "before the first course."

His fondness for latte and antipasto antedates their widespread popularity.

Anticipate: A verb meaning to take action beforehand. Described by Paul Lovinger as a "wounded word," *anticipate* should be used only in this sense, not as a synonym for *expect*.

The chess master anticipated his opponent's every move.

Anxious, Eager: Use *anxious* where there is a sense of anxiety, *eager* where there is pleasant expectation.

> The grandmother awaited the birth of her first grandchild anxiously; she was eager to hold the baby in her arms.

Apt, Liable, Likely, Prone: *Apt* implies a natural tendency (*I am apt to forget their names*). *Liable* suggests the possibility or probability of risk (*The theme of the ad campaign is liable to be misunderstood*). *Likely* conveys simple probability (*The forecast says rain is likely*). *Prone* means tending (*People who are accident-prone have a tendency to fall often or to cut themselves with sharp knives.*)

A While, Awhile: *While* means a period of time; *awhile* means *for* a period of time. Thus, to write "I will be gone for awhile" is to double up on the word *for*. Write "I will be gone for a while" or "I will be gone awhile."

Bad, Badly: To help you decide which of these two words to use, substitute another adjective or adverb for *bad* or *badly* in the sentence. For example, in the sentence "I feel bad (or badly) about the results," substitute the adjective *unhappy* and the adverb *unhappily*.

> I feel unhappy/unhappily about the results.

Clearly, you wouldn't write "I feel unhappily"; therefore, choose the adjective and write "I feel bad."

Beside, Besides: When you mean "next to," use *beside*; when you mean "in addition to" or "except for," use *besides*.

Besides the defense attorney, no one was willing to sit beside the prisoner.

Better/Best; Worse/Worst: When you're comparing the merits of two things or people, use *better* (or *worse*); when comparing three or more, use *best* (or *worst*).

Between, Among: An ill-founded rule calls for using *between* with two items and *among* with more than two. Doggedly following this rule can lead you into such an absurdity as *She traveled among Santa Fe, Taos, and Albuquerque*. A better rule is to use *between* when individual relationships are emphasized and the number is unspecified *(he appeared between acts; cooperation between neighboring countries)*, and when repetition is implied *(sobbing between breaths)*. Use *among* with unspecified numbers if individual relationships are not emphasized *(discontent among the employees)*. You are probably on safe ground using whichever word sounds right. The following examples illustrate choices that sound right.

The anthropologist traveled among the Navajo and Hopi.

She traveled between Rome, Paris, and Berlin.

Watch out for illogical constructions that include the word *each* or *every: He was sobbing between each breath*.

Bi-, Semi-: If you want to avoid confusion when referring to a period of time, consider abandoning the use of the prefixes *bi* and *semi* and say every two weeks, every two months, twice a year—or whatever interval you are describing.

Billion: Means a thousand million (1,000,000,000) in the United States but a million million (1,000,000,000,000) in the United Kingdom. Where appropriate for your audience, specify which meaning you're using.

> three billion (U.S.)
> 1.5 billion (U.K.)

Can, May: The rule that distinguishes between *can* (the ability or power to do something) and *may* (permission to do it) is weakening. The *Harper Dictionary of Contemporary Usage* considers this "rather a pity, for the distinction is a nice one—and not really very hard to remember." Formal usage still requires the use of *may* for permission, despite the prevalence of *can* for *may* in speech.

Capital, Capitol: *Capital* refers to wealth, the city that is the seat of government, or an uppercase letter. *Capitol* is the building in which state or federal officials congregate. The *Capitol*, when referring to the home of the U.S. Congress, is always capitalized.

capital C
(*upper case*)

capital
(*money*)

capitol
(*building*)

People who work in the Capitol disburse a great deal of the taxpayers' capital.

 Only <u>o</u>ne building in the U.S. is the Capit<u>o</u>l, and only <u>o</u>ne building in each state is its capit<u>o</u>l; <u>a</u>ll others are capit<u>a</u>l.

Complement, Compliment: *Complement* is both a verb and a noun, meaning to complete a whole or satisfy a need. *Compliment* also functions as both verb and noun, meaning praise.

Her efforts <u>complemented</u> those of the rest of the team.
               verb

A <u>complement</u> of twelve laborers performed the task.
    noun

She <u>complimented</u> him on the apple pie he had baked.
      verb

Her <u>compliment</u> was sincere.
    noun

Nowadays we are all of us so hard up that the only pleasant things to pay are compliments.—Oscar Wilde

Comprise: Means to include or be made up of; therefore, *comprised of* is redundant. It is frequently confused with *compose* or incorrectly used as a synonym for *constitute*. The traditional dictum is that the whole comprises the parts; the parts constitute the whole. If *comprise* sounds stilted, substitute *is composed of*.

Wrong: High-tech companies comprise only 10 percent of GNP.

Right: High-tech companies constitute only 10 percent of GNP.

Right: The company comprises three divisions.

 If you can substitute *include* for *comprise*, you are using *comprise* correctly.

Contact: This word seems to have made the complete transition to respectability as a verb, but I might still look for a more descriptive alternative.

Continual, Continuous: *Continual* means over and over again; *continuous* means uninterrupted or unbroken. Dictionaries now list these words as synonymous, but maintaining the distinction between them helps preserve the richness of our vocabulary.

Since he coughed continually, the doctor kept him under continuous observation.

A man's memory may almost become the art of continually varying and misrepresenting his past, according to his interests in the present.—George Santayana

Convince, Persuade: Though the meaning of these words is similar (to bring to belief), each has a preferred usage. You persuade someone to do something, but you convince someone about something. In other words, *convince…of*, but *persuade… to/that/as to/about*.

> He convinced me of his sincerity.
>
> He persuaded me that she was sincere.
>
> She persuaded me to attend the meeting.

Cope: Careful usage limits *cope* to coping *with* something, not just coping.

Council, Counsel, Consul: *Council*, always a noun, refers to an assemblage of persons or a committee. *Counsel* has both verb and noun forms, meaning to advise, the advice itself, or an attorney.

> Counsel for the defense counseled her client not to speak to the council members; the council resented her counsel.

Consul is a person in the foreign service who represents the business interests of the country.

Cum: A recently popular way to indicate a coupling, as in *bookstore-cum-coffeeshop*. As with many word fads, this one is easily overdone.

Data: A plural Latin word meaning information, especially in numerical form. Acceptance of *data* as a singular is widespread, and it has all but eliminated use of the Latin singular *datum*. However, in scientific and formal writing, the plural form is still preferred.

> Data are… (*not* Data is…)

Decimate, Annihilate: The literal meaning of *decimate* is to destroy one-tenth of, though it is sometimes loosely used to mean to destroy a large part of. *Annihilate* means to destroy completely (thus, *annihilate completely* is redundant). The words *decimate* and *annihilate* are not interchangeable.

Different from, Different than: *Different from* is preferred in most cases, especially if it is followed by a single noun, pronoun, or short phrase.

> His writing style is different from mine.

Different than is acceptable if it avoids wordiness or is followed by a clause.

> **Wordy:** Writing style today is different from what it was a century ago.

> **Better:** Writing style today is different than a century ago.

Dilemma, Predicament, Hobson's Choice: Reserve the use of *dilemma* for a choice between two equal alternatives; to refer to a difficult situation, use such words as *predicament*, *plight*, or *problem*. *Hobson's choice* is the apparent freedom of choice when there is no real alternative; it is named for Thomas Hobson, a seventeenth-century liveryman who gave customers the choice of the horse next to the stable door or no horse at all.

Disburse, Disperse: *Disburse* means to pay out, as from a fund; *disperse* means to scatter.

> He disbursed the proceeds of the estate after he had dispersed the ashes.

Discreet, Discrete: *Discreet* describes behavior that is prudent or respectful of propriety. *Discrete* frequently has a scientific connotation and means separate, distinct, or individual.

> She made discreet inquiries into his whereabouts.

> The smooth surface of water seems to contradict the discrete nature of its molecules.

Disinterested, Uninterested: Cautious writers still observe the distinction between these two words. *Disinterested* means objective or impartial, not influenced by personal advantage. *Uninterested* means indifferent or lacking interest in an outcome.

> A disinterested scientist is not uninterested in the outcome of her experiments.

Due to, Because of: Though used interchangeably in informal writing, careful writers will use *because of* to indicate a cause-and-effect relationship and reserve *due to* for use after forms of the verb *to be*.

> The driver lost control of the car because of faulty brakes.

> The collision was due to faulty brakes.

Ecology: The study of the relationship between organisms and their environment. Often misused as a synonym for *environment*, which means surroundings.

Emigrate, Immigrate: To *emigrate* is to leave one's country permanently; thus one emigrates **from** a country. To *immigrate* is to move to a new country permanently; thus one immigrates **to** a country.

Eminent, Imminent, Emanate: *Eminent* means well known or distinguished; *imminent* means about to happen; *emanate* means to originate or issue forth.

The arrival of the eminent statesman was imminent.

A light emanated from the shuttered windows.

Enthused: A "back formation" from the word *enthusiasm* (as *donate* was derived from *donation*), *enthused* is not yet acceptable in formal writing. Use *enthusiastic*.

Farther, Further:

Traditional American usage calls for *farther* when actual physical distance is involved (*We walked farther than we had intended*). Use *further* in the sense of more or additional (*further deliberation, going further into debt*) and in the figurative sense of distance (*We are moving further from the truth*).

Fewer, Less: *Fewer* is used with individual items that can be counted *(fewer potatoes)*; *less* is used for quantity or bulk, when the item is regarded as a single entity *(less oatmeal)*.

> The fewer mistakes you make, the less embarrassment you will feel.

> A diet that has less fat will also have fewer calories.

Less takes a singular verb and *fewer* a plural one.

> Less fat is needed if fewer calories are to be consumed.

Finalize: Resistance to this word because of its bureaucratic flavor appears to be waning, perhaps because substitutes are wordy *(to put in final form)* or fail to convey the same meaning *(conclude, complete)*. Nonetheless, *-ize* words such as *finalize* and *prioritize* create an inelegant patina that you might want to avoid in formal writing.

Flammable, Inflammable: Both mean capable of burning. Because of the danger that *inflammable* will be mistaken for not flammable, use *flammable* to mean combustible and *nonflammable* for its antonym.

Flaunt, Flout: A common error is to use *flaunt*, which means to show off, for *flout*, which means to show contempt. Although sometimes widespread errors evolve into acceptability, confusing these two words is simply an error.

> Even in an academic setting, he flaunted his superior knowledge.

> They tried to flout U.S. tax laws by establishing offshore accounts.

Foreword, Forward: Mixing up these two words is a serious blunder, especially in large print at the front of a book. *Foreword* is a preface or introductory note. It deals with w<u>o</u>rds and is spelled with an o. *Forward* is the opposite of backward and means at or near the front, or moving in the direction of the front. There is no such word as *foreward*.

Fulsome: Modern usage limits the meaning of *fulsome* to offensively excessive or insincere; disgusting. This word is often used incorrectly to mean abundant or lavish. Don't write *fulsome praise* unless you wish to be uncomplimentary.

Gender, Sex: *Gender* is a grammatical term that classifies words as feminine, masculine, or neuter. In recent years, it has been increasingly used as a euphemism for *sex* when identifying whether a person or animal is male or female. When filling out forms nowadays, you may be asked for age, income, and gender. As Paul Lovinger says, "It is not obvious why *sex*, in such an innocent sense, needs a euphemism." But for now, it seems *gender* will be used to indicate sex and *sex* to indicate the sexual act or sexual activity.

Get, Got: Although *get* and *got* can claim a long history of use in the English language, careful writers will avoid their casual overtones by substituting words such as *have* or *receive* whenever possible.

> I've got the answer. (I have the answer.)
>
> We've got to comply. (We have to comply *or* We must comply.)

In some cases, *got* remains a suitable choice.

They got what they deserve.

Heighth: A non-word. The correct word is *height*.

Home, Hone: The verb *hone*, meaning to sharpen, is sometimes incorrectly substituted for *home* in the expression *home in*, meaning to be guided to a target.

Wrong: He honed in on the target.

Right: He honed his skills in order to earn a promotion.

Right: The airplane homed in on the runway.

Homogeneous, Homogenous: *Homogeneous* means uniform in structure or composition throughout. *Homogenous* is correctly used in biology to indicate a correspondence between organs or parts that are related by common descent. However, it appears more often as a misspelling or mispronunciation of *homogeneous*.

Hopefully: This adverb means full of hope (*He uttered his prayer hopefully and fervently*). The more common usage today is in place of "I hope" (*Hopefully, I will receive a raise*). A great deal of ink has been spent trying to forestall acceptance of *hopefully* in the latter sense. But just as *happily, presumably*, and *luckily* have been accepted as standard usage, *hopefully* may someday cease to grate on the nerves of traditionalists. For now, a strong case can be made for avoiding the word simply because it is overworked. I *hope* I make myself clear!

I, Me, Myself: *I* is the subjective case and thus should be used when it is the subject of a sentence (the *who* or *what* the rest of the sentence is about).

> My brother and I went to the ball game.

Me is the objective case and should be used when it is the object of the action or thought conveyed by the verb of the sentence, or when it is the object of a preposition.

> Between you and me, I hate Sunday afternoon football.

> Ebenezer invited Elijah and me to the opera.

In a sentence such as the last, if you remove "Elijah and," it is obvious that *me* is the correct pronoun.

Myself is correctly used for emphasis (*I, myself, will see to it*) or as a reflexive (*I hurt myself falling from the roof*). Do not use *myself* as a substitute for *I* or *me*.

> **Wrong:** The money was given to my partner and myself.
> **Right:** The money was given to my partner and me.

> **Wrong:** My partner and myself are seeking underwriting for a business venture.
> **Right:** My partner and I are seeking underwriting for a business venture.

Impact: A noun meaning violent contact, as of two objects striking each other. Do not use it as a substitute for *effect, influence*, or *result*. As a verb, it's a poor substitute for *affect*.

Imply, Infer: To *imply* is to suggest directly or insinuate; to *infer* is to draw a conclusion or deduce.

> I infer from your remark that no threat was implied.

Insure, Ensure, Assure: All three words mean to make secure or certain.

Victory is assured. (*or* ensured *or* insured)

Assure has the meaning of setting someone's mind at rest. Both *ensure* and *insure* mean to make secure from harm. Only *insure* should be used regarding guaranteeing of life or property against risk.

Irregardless: A redundancy. Use *regardless*.

It's, Its: *It's* is the contraction of *it is* or *it has*. *Its* is a possessive pronoun. (See p. 48.)

Lay, Lie: *Lay* is a transitive verb (i.e., it takes an object); it means to place or put down. The past tense and past participle form is *laid*.

> Lay the package on the table. (**package** is the object of the verb **lay**)

Lie is an intransitive verb (i.e., it does not take an object); it means to recline. The past tense of *lie* is *lay*; the past participle is *lain*.

> Lie on your exercise mat.

> He lay on the mat for half an hour.

> He had lain on the mat for half an hour when I arrived.

 To help you decide whether to use *lay* or *lie*, substitute the word *place*. If *place* sounds right, use *lay*.

Lend, Loan: Call me old-fashioned, but I still prefer to distinguish between the verb *lend* and the noun *loan*. Doesn't "I will lend you my pen" seem more elegant than "I will loan you my pen"? Despite its widespread acceptance as a verb, I will continue to use *loan* only as a noun (*I received a $1,000 loan*).

Like, As: *Like* is correct when used as a preposition (in other words, when it's followed by a noun or pronoun).

> She writes like Hemingway.

> *My Luv is like a red, red rose.*—Robert Burns

Like is also acceptable when it introduces a clause from which the verb has been omitted.

> He took to politics like a fish to water.

In formal writing, substitute *as* or *as if* for *like* when it's used as a conjunction.

> Residents of the model village live <u>as</u> the villagers did two hundred years ago.

> The shareholder spoke <u>as if</u> he had privileged information.

In journalism and informal writing, *like* is often used as a conjunction.

> Sales aren't growing like they were a decade ago.

Literally: Although a *literal translation* is word for word and exact, *literally* has strayed into being used for emphasis in ways that are anything but literal. Your credibility is jeopardized if you write "We were literally climbing the walls." On the other hand, you might write "He literally got away with murder" and mean it if he killed someone and got away with it. Use *literally* with care.

Loose, Lose: *Loose* is an adjective meaning unrestrained or not fastened. *Lose* is a verb that is the antonym of *win* and *find*.

Majority, Plurality: A *majority* is at least half of the votes cast plus one; a *plurality* is the highest number of votes when there are three or more candidates.

Meantime, Meanwhile: *Meantime* is a noun that refers to an interval between events.

> We will meet at 3:00 this afternoon. In the meantime, prepare your responses to the board's questions.

Meanwhile is an adverb meaning *during* the intervening time.

> Meanwhile, back at the ranch...

You can interchange *in the meantime* and *meanwhile*, but do not write "in the meanwhile."

Media: A newspaper is a medium of mass communication. So are radio, television, and magazines. As a group, it is correct to refer to them as "the media," but be sure to use a plural verb: *media are*. If fortune tellers or a substance used in a lab to culture cells is the kind of medium being discussed, *mediums* is the correct plural.

Myriad: An adjective meaning a large number. Don't write "a myriad of."

Myself: See the entry for I, Me, Myself, p. 139.

Nano-: A prefix meaning billionth or one part in one billion (U.S.). *Nano-* is a scientific term that has been seized upon by nonscientists and often used (incorrectly) to indicate a very small amount *(I didn't consider the alternative for a nanosecond)*. Let's leave *nano-* to the scientists.

Nauseated, Nauseous: According to Theodore Bernstein, a person who feels sick is no more nauseous than a person who has been poisoned is poisonous. Though the distinction between the verb *nauseate* and the adjective *nauseous* has all but disappeared in speech, you should observe the difference in writing. Something that makes you feel sick is *nauseous* *(nauseous fumes)*; what you feel is *nauseated (The fumes nauseated me)*.

People, Persons: In general, use *people* for larger groups, *persons* for an exact or small number.

Eight persons are being held as hostages.

The trouble with people is not that they don't know but that they know so much that ain't so.—Josh Billings

If *persons* sounds affected, try using a more specific noun, such as *commuters*, *residents*, or *visitors*.

Pore, Pour: The verb *pore* means reading or scrutinizing intently, and *pour* means to let flow. The noun *pore* is a minute surface opening, as in the skin of an animal.

While she was poring over the document, she poured herself a glass of wine.

Predominant, Predominate: *Predominant* is an adjective meaning most common or having the greatest influence or force. *Predominate* is a verb meaning to prevail or to have the greatest influence.

> The predominant theme of the parade was patriotism.

> The patriotic theme predominated over all others.

Though the adverb *predominantly* is correct, there is no such word as *predominately*.

Principal, Principle: *Principal* functions as both noun and adjective. The noun refers to the head of a school or firm, or to capital that earns interest; the adjective means chief or main. *Principle* is a noun meaning rule or standard.

> The principal's principal principle was "Be Prepared for Anything."

Rebut, Refute: The verb *rebut* means to argue against; *refute* to prove incorrect.

Respectfully, Respectively: *Respectfully* means full of respect (*I respectfully disagree*). It may be used in the formal closing of a letter (*Respectfully yours*). *Respectively* means individually in the order given (*Suzanne Johnson and William Campbell were elected president and vice-president, respectively*). Do not sign a letter "Respectively yours."

Shall, Will: This is one instance where the fading of an old grammatical distinction is welcome. Don't worry about rules regarding *shall* and *will*, or *should* and *would*. Just let your ear be your guide.

Stanch, Staunch: *Stanch* means to stop the flow; *staunch* is steadfast, true.

> You may need a staunch friend to stanch a bloody wound.

Stationary, Stationery: *Stationary* means fixed in position, not moving. *Stationery* is writing paper and envelopes.

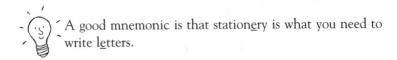 A good mnemonic is that station**e**ry is what you need to write l**e**tters.

Tenant, Tenet: Although both words derive from Latin *tenere* (meaning "to hold") and to the untrained ear may sound similar, the meanings do not overlap. A *tenant* is one who temporarily holds or occupies property (land, buildings). A *tenet* is an opinion or principle held by a person or organization.

> The tenants' association drew up a list of tenets for their organization.

That: As an adverb, *that* means to such an extent or degree. *That* is correctly used if what it refers to is clear (*I won't buy a car that old*). A statement such as "I'm not that hungry" is colloquial unless it follows something like "John ate twelve pancakes."

That, Which: Generally, use *that* to introduce restrictive, or defining, clauses; use *which* to introduce nonrestrictive clauses. (See p. 62.)

> **Restrictive:** The pencil that needs sharpening is on my desk.

Nonrestrictive: The pencil, which needs sharpening, is on my desk.

In the restrictive sentence, the pencil is one of several and thus must be further identified; in the nonrestrictive sentence, there is only one pencil, and by the way, it needs sharpening. Note that commas are omitted with restrictive phrases.

Restrictive: *I try to leave out the parts that people skip.*
—Elmore Leonard

Nonrestrictive: *Dr. Seuss is remembered for the murder of Dick and Jane, <u>which</u> was a mercy killing of the highest order.*—Anna Quindlen

In the following example, *which* might refer to the word *taxes* or to the entire preceding phrase. Rewrite to avoid such ambiguity.

Unclear: Any attempts to increase taxes, which would harm the recovery...

Clear: Since any attempts to increase taxes would harm the recovery...

 Whenever you write *which*, try substituting *that*. If it doesn't alter the meaning, *that* is probably the better word to use.

That, Who, Whose: Although in earlier versions of *Write Right!* I observed that the rules governing the choice between

that and *who* had been relaxed, I now think we've gone over-board. *That* threatens to obliterate *who*. Using *who* to refer to persons makes them seem more human, and we need all the help we can get in that direction these days. Use *that* to refer to things.

Poor: The students that met me in the classroom…

Better: The students who met me in the classroom…

Use *whose* to refer either to persons or things.

The crowd, whose patience had worn thin…

The building, whose architect won a national award…

There's: The contagion of using the contracted form of *there is* with a plural word has spread from spoken to written language. It's an error whether in speech or writing.

Wrong: There's three reasons…

Right: There are three reasons…

Was, Were: Use *were* when expressing a wish or a condition contrary to fact and when following the words *as if* and *as though*. (See p. 16.)

The silence made it seem as if he were speaking to an empty room.

If it were not for the presents, an elopement would be preferable.—George Ade

Use *was* when expressing a past condition that is not contrary to fact.

If Hortense was guilty, she did not show it.

Whatever, Wherever, Whoever, Whenever: Should they be one word or two? If it's a statement, one word; if it's a question, two.

He does whatever he wants.

What ever made you say that?

Who, Whom:

The irony of the *who/whom* problem is that some avoid *whom* completely because they feel uncertain how to use it.

Wrong: Who does this belong to?

Others use it where it doesn't belong, mistakenly thinking they are being grammatically correct.

Wrong: Whom do you think you are?

The best guide is to substitute a personal pronoun for *who* or *whom*. If *he*, *she*, or *they* fits, use *who* (nominative case); if *him*, *her*, or *them* fits, use *whom* (objective case).

The man who committed the crime...
(**he** committed the crime)

Whom the gods wish to destroy, they first call promising.
—Cyril Connolly   (the gods wish to destroy **them**)

To whom shall I report?   (to **him**, **her**, or **them**)

For prying into any human affairs, none are equal to those whom it does not concern.—Victor Hugo
(it does not concern **them**)

An acquaintance is a person whom we know well enough to borrow from, but not well enough to lend to.
—Ambrose Bierce   (we know **him** well enough)

People who say they sleep like a baby usually don't have one.—Leo J. Burke   (**they** say)

Paul Brians (see Web Sites, p. 200) suggests that you use *who* if you're still uncertain after trying this replacement test. "You'll bother fewer people and have a fair chance of being right."

Would of: Incorrect usage. Write "would have."

I would have (*not* would of) been on time if I hadn't had a flat tire.

Wreak, Wreck: To *wreak* is to inflict; it is correctly used with *havoc*. To *wreck* is to destroy, so *to wreck havoc* is incorrect. (*To reek havoc* would also be incorrect.)

> *Our affinity for language makes us human. We are never better than when we use words clearly, eloquently, and civilly.*—David W. Orr

6 Style

> To make our words count for as much as
> possible is surely the simplest as well as
> the hardest secret of style.
> —Wilson Follett

The word *style* means everything from conventions of punctuation and capitalization to how written words convey the writer's personality. I use the term in this chapter to suggest ways to make writing readable and ideas clear.

First, let's take a look at the style that dominates the Internet. With its emphasis on speed and up-to-the-minute currency, online style is the ultimate insider's jargon. Rather than make their writing accessible to the masses, online stylists use language as a gatekeeper: "If you're one of us, you'll be able to handle it," seems to be their view.

But even within this in-your-face, elitist approach, a set of commandments has evolved. These rules embrace the irreverent and the colloquial. They encourage the use of initialisms (FWIW, B2B, LOL) and the creation of imaginative new words: *microserfs* (Microsoft employees), *infobahn* (the information superhighway), and *digerati* (the digital elite).

Online style is beyond the scope of this book. If you work or study within its sphere of influence, you should probably become familiar with the rules enunciated on Web sites and in books on the subject. (See Bibliography.)

Think Before You Write

Writing proceeds more smoothly if you pause before plunging in.

- What do you want to say?

- Who will read it?

Keep coming back to those two elements (message and audience) as you write. Ask yourself if readers will grasp what you've written.

> It's impossible for a muddy thinker to write good English.—William Zinsser

"Think of it as elevator talk." That's the advice given to Stanford students learning to write about their work. Someone in an elevator asks what your research is about, and you have to respond in the time it takes to go from the lobby to the fifth floor.

This approach changed one student's paper from "Investigating Cytoskeletal Dynamics in the Development of Epithelial Cell Polarity" into "How Do Cells Know Up from Down?"

Dense, awkward writing detracts from what you want to convey. Confusing writing bogs readers down. Clear, concise writing, on the other hand, speeds readers along.

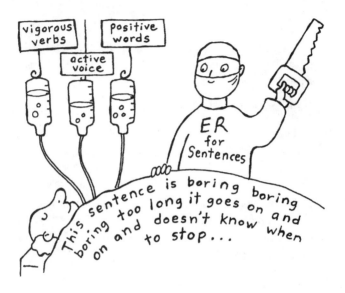

Omit Unnecessary Words

> If it is possible to cut a word out, always
> cut it out.—George Orwell

This rule is increasingly important because word processors encourage verbosity. However, the technology that spreads the disease also provides the cure; revising on a word processor is relatively simple.

Impressive writing doesn't come from long words strung together in convoluted sentences. Writing that's hard to understand is just poorly written, not profound.

> **Wordy:** Our proposal follows the sequential itemization of points occurring elsewhere in your Request for Proposal, wherever possible, to facilitate your review.

> **Translation:** We will follow your outline.

Redundancy and sloppy usage are widespread (see the list of redundant expressions on page 157). "General consensus of opinion" uses four words where only one is correct (*consensus* means collective opinion or general agreement). "Close proximity" is one word too many, since *proximity* means close to. Watch for repetitions in acronyms as well. Write "SAT," not "SAT test," and "ATM," not "ATM machine." The V in HIV stands for virus; the non-redundant phrase is "AIDS virus."

> *The equivalent of junk food for the writer is redundancy, and the job of the editor is to count calories and impose diets.*
> —Bruce O. Boston

REDUNDANT EXPRESSIONS

added bonus	past history
advance warning	present incumbent
both men and women alike	rarely ever
current status	refer back
end result	regular routine
extra added features	small in size
first time ever	sudden impulse
future plans	sum total
hot water heater	temporary reprieve
join together	tired cliché
joint collaboration	two polar opposites
limited only to	ultimate outcome
may possibly	unexpected surprise
natural instinct	various different
original founder	10 a.m. Friday morning

Think about the meaning of a word. *Unanimous* means having agreement and consent of all; what is added by writing *completely unanimous*? Clutter. How about the ubiquitous *free gift*. Is there any other kind?

Wordy: She estimated attendance at around 500.
Better: She estimated attendance at 500.

Wordy: Chances are that you have probably heard of...
Better: Chances are that you have heard of...
or You have probably heard of...

> *Wherever we can make twenty-five words*
> *do the work of fifty, we halve the area in which*
> *looseness and disorganization can flourish.*
> —Wilson Follett

To make twenty-five words do the work of fifty, cut the unnecessary words. Avoid the following redundancies:

- The word *rather* in a sentence with another comparative

  Wordy: It would be safer to destroy the chemicals rather than to store them.
  Better: It would be safer to destroy the chemicals than to store them.

- Leisurely openers such as *There is*, *There are*, and *It is significant to note that*

  Wordy: There is some evidence that suggests...
  Better: Some evidence suggests...

- *As well as* when used with *both*

  Wordy: The press release was mailed both to employees as well as shareholders.
  Better: The press release was mailed both to employees and to shareholders.

Trim wordy expressions.

Wordy	Trimmed
it is often the case that	frequently
fail to comply with	violate
in the event that	if
be of the opinion that	believe
be in possession of	have
owing to the fact that	since (*or* because)
the fact that he had arrived	his arrival
on the order of	about
in advance of	before
in spite of the fact that	although
is indicative of	indicates
had occasion to be	was
put in an appearance	appeared
take into consideration	consider
each and every	each (*or* every)

The best cure for wordiness is to revise. Then go back and revise again. Edit once strictly for spare words. When you think you have pruned every one, look again to see if you missed any. Sometimes when you've stripped a sentence of its padding, you discover that the whole sentence is devoid of ideas and thus expendable.

> *He can compress the most words into the smallest idea of any man I ever met.*
> —Abraham Lincoln

Use Simple Words

Why write "facilitate his departure" when you can write "help him leave"? Does *functionality* mean anything other than *function*? *Specific outcomes and objectives* are probably *goals*. Avoid fancy words and phrases when simpler, more direct ones convey the idea.

Stilted: Per our aforementioned discussion, I am herewith enclosing a copy of...
Simple: As promised, here is a copy of...

Poor: I'll contact you to finalize the agreement.
Better: I'll call at your office to sign the contract.

If the following words appear often in your writing, replace them with their simpler counterparts.

Stuffy	Simple
utilize	use
ameliorate	improve
modification	change
deficiency	lack
preventative	preventive
methodology	method
subsequent to	after

> Shortening a passage isn't merely a matter of taking words away, but of making sure the remaining words are the right ones—words that do enough work to earn their keep.—Jack Lynch

Write with Strong Verbs and in the Active Voice

Strong verbs "earn their keep." Pass up colorless verbs in favor of lively ones.

Colorless	Lively
exhibit a tendency to	tend to
conduct an investigation	investigate
make a comparison between	compare
perform an assessment of	assess

The difference between active and passive voice is the difference between *Karen read the report* and *The report was read by Karen*. In the active voice, the subject acts (*Karen read*) instead of being acted upon (*The report was read by...*). The passive voice is wordy and lacks the vigor of the active voice. Changing a sentence from passive to active usually improves it.

Active　　　　　　　*Passive*

Passive: Hazardous chemicals should never be poured into the sink.
Active: Never pour hazardous chemicals into the sink.

Passive: The collision was witnessed by a pedestrian.
Active: A pedestrian saw the collision.

Use the passive voice in the following situations:

- When the thing acted upon is more important than the person performing the action

  The meeting was canceled.

- In technical material

  The test apparatus was divided into two zones.

- Where anonymity of those performing the action is appropriate or unavoidable

  The information was leaked to the press.

Choose the Right "Person" for Your Audience

A decision that's closely related to active or passive voice is whether to write in the first person (*I, we*) or the more impersonal third person (*he, she, they*). And should you address the reader as "you" (second person)?

These questions don't have one-response-fits-all answers. In its favor, first-person writing encourages use of the active voice and avoids awkward substitutes for *I* (such as *the author*). Third-person writing puts the writer in the background, which may be appropriate in certain writing; it also avoids being overly familiar.

Readers of scientific or technical writing, where the emphasis is on results, tend to expect an impersonal third-person approach. First-person writing may deflect the reader's attention from the message to the messenger.

Other kinds of writing may call for the more friendly, human tone of first-person writing. This book is an example of first- and second-person writing. What I present is *my* advice, and I'm talking to *you*! Let the nature of the writing and of the audience determine your choice.

Use a Positive Form

Stating things positively starts the reader on the right foot. Watch for the word *not* and see if you can restate the idea more effectively.

Negative: He often did not arrive on time.
Positive: He often arrived late.

Negative: The witness did not speak during the inquest.
Positive: The witness was silent during the inquest.

Try replacing a word or phrase plus *not* with its antonym.

Negative	Positive
did not remember	forgot
was not present	was absent
did not pay attention to	ignored

Reserve the negative form for those instances where it produces the desired effect.

Of all noises, I think music is the least disagreeable.
—Samuel Johnson

I have always been in a condition in which I cannot not write.—Barbara Tuchman

Be Specific and Concrete

Use examples to bring abstract ideas down to earth.

> **Abstract:** The equipment malfunctioned.
> **Concrete:** The camera failed to expose any film.

> **Abstract:** The new health and family programs improved employee performance.
> **Concrete:** Absenteeism was reduced by 40 percent when the company built an employee gym and offered child-care services.

Wherever possible, replace abstract words with concrete ones. Help readers visualize what you're writing about.

Abstract	Concrete
vehicle	bicycle, panel truck
food	pizza, papaya
color	red, chartreuse
emotion	hatred, confusion

Vary Your Sentences

Use sentences of different lengths and types to retain reader interest and to provide relief from monotonous declarative sentences. Open with one of the following:

- With a subordinate clause

  If you want to be a writer, don't listen to any advice given by writers.—Jon Scieszka

  When the student is ready, the teacher will appear.
  —Chinese proverb

- With an infinitive

  To get profit without risk, experience without danger, and reward without work is as impossible as it is to live without being born.—A. P. Gouthey

- With a participial phrase

  Thrusting my nose firmly between his teeth, I threw him heavily to the ground on top of me.—Mark Twain

- With a preposition

  Behind the phony tinsel of Hollywood lies the real tinsel. —Oscar Levant

Notice the rhythm of what you have written. Is it choppy, lively, flowing? Listen to the sound of the words—are there any awkward neighbors like *Our products produced...* or *prevention intervention*? Use rhythm, flow, and contrast to make language and meaning harmonious. Read what you have written out loud; you will discover awkward passages and places where punctuation is needed.

Use Intensifiers with Care

We sometimes rely on the word *very* to convey a strong emotion or lean on words like *incredible* or *unbelievable* to describe a powerful experience. Such words signal sloppy writing—and sloppy thinking. Indeed, intensifier-heavy writing may actually weaken the emotion you wish to convey.

Poor: His contribution was very critical.

Better: His contribution was critical.

Absolute words such as *unique* and *final* stand by themselves; you do not make them more emphatic by adding the word *very*. If a word seems weak without *very*, use another word that doesn't require such buttressing.

Weak	Strong
very stubborn	obstinate, bullheaded
very weak	frail, feeble, fragile
very surprised	astonished, astounded, amazed
very angry	livid, incensed, irate

If you write that something was "incredible," you probably mean that it was amazing or top-notch, not that it was unthinkable or not to be believed. From its origin as a word meaning not to be believed, *incredible* has strayed far afield. It's now loosely used to express amazement—even admiration—rather than skepticism. With a little thought or a look in your thesaurus, you can find a word that comes closer to your meaning.

To describe the extraordinary, focus on what makes it so. Steer clear of words that say what it *isn't* in favor of words that say what it *is*.

Appeal to the senses: how the salsa nips the tongue or the modern concerto assaults the ears. Allow its distinguishing features to evoke an image.

In autumn, rains return and with them silky verdant grasses, nothing like the color of spring, but a lush, rampant green that makes you understand the urge horses must have to graze. When the trees begin to splatter yellow, russet, bronze, and scarlet over the slopes, the air sharpens to a noon clarity that outlines every leaf.

I wish I could limn the autumn sunsets. Words sound too exaggerated because a literal shower of gold seems to fall over the valley, as if in a myth, forming a veil between me, with my feet on the solid ground, and the glob of live lava sinking in the western distance. The sky goes wild with colors—opal, saffron, dusty blue, copper, ash, blood. …I hesitate to go on about sunset, that hackneyed oil painting. If only the townspeople would gather at the Porta Colonia parking lot looking out over the valley and give a standing ovation. (Frances Mayes, *In Tuscany*)

Not an *incredible* in the whole passage.

There are legitimate uses of words that express incredulity. If you want to cast doubt on the integrity of a witness or the results of an experiment, you might write about the *incredible testimony* or *unbelievable results*. Legitimate uses of the word *very* also exist, though none come to me at the moment. But do take the time to figure out what you want to say, and choose words that will help you say it.

Edit for Bias

Bias-free language avoids possible offense by substituting alternative terminology. Here are a few guidelines to remove bias from your writing without resorting to awkward wording.

- Do not mention race, gender, age, or disability unless it is pertinent.

- Avoid stereotypes and labels.

- Give parallel treatment (Mr. Waxman and Ms. Stone, *not* Mr. Waxman and Linda).

- Find substitutes for words that may be considered insensitive or confusing, such as masculine pronouns. (See p. 37.)

More detailed suggestions for avoiding bias are presented in two of my books, *Better Letters* and *Rewrite Right!* (see the bibliography).

Become Your Reader

> *I don't think it ever hurts the writer to sort of stand back now and then and look at his stuff as if he were reading it instead of writing it.*—James Jones

Have you brought readers along, step by step? If you present too much information too quickly, readers balk. Build on common ground, on a premise that everyone understands. Proceed from there with digestible bits.

Here's how one writer tackled a difficult subject:

> It was about elementary arithmetic, to begin with, and it was not until the second chapter that I as much as got into Arabic numerals, and not until the fourth chapter that I got to fractions. However, by the end of the book I was talking about imaginary numbers, hyperimaginary numbers, and transfinite numbers—and that was the real purpose of the book. In going from counting to transfinites, I followed such

a careful and gradual plan that it never stopped seeming easy. (Isaac Asimov, *Opus 100*)

Revisit the questions you asked yourself when starting to write. Have you said what you wanted to say? Did you use as few words as possible? Will your readers still be with you at the end? If your answers are all positive, congratulate yourself on a job well done.

Resources

Frequently Misspelled Words

To differentiate between words with similar sounds (*accept/except*), a brief parenthetical definition follows the first entry. The sound-alike is indented below and then defined at its own alphabetical entry.

Necessary definitions or alternative spellings follow some entries. A list of plurals of foreign words appears at the end of this section.

A

aberration
abridgment
absence
accelerator
accept (receive)
  except
accessible
accessory

accumulate
achievement
acknowledgment
acquiesce
acquittal
adjourn
adolescence
advertisement

aerosol
affidavit
aging
algorithm
align
allotment
allotted
all right

already
anachronism
analogous
analysis
ancillary
anesthetic
annihilate
anomaly
anonymous
antecedent

antihistamine
apartheid
aperture
apparatus
apparel
appraisal
apropos
arctic
arraign
arteriosclerosis

arthritis
asphyxiate
aspirin
assessor
asterisk
attendance
attorneys
autumn
auxiliary

B

balance
ballistic
balloon
bankruptcy
barbiturate
basically
beneficial
benign
bereave
bilateral

bilingual
binary
biodegradable
biopsy
bipartisan
blatant
bloc (group)
bouillon (soup)
   bullion
bourgeois

boutique
boycott
braille
brief
bruise
bullion (gold)
   bouillon
bureaucracy
business
byte

C

caffeine
calendar
calorie
campaign
cannot
captain
carat

carbohydrate
carburetor
Caribbean
carriage
Caucasian
caucus
caveat

ceiling
cellar
cemetery
censor
census
centimeter
centrifugal

cerebral
certain
changeable
charisma
chassis
chauvinist
chiropractor
chlorophyll
chocolate
cholesterol
Christian
Cincinnati
cipher
circuit
cite (quote)
   sight
   site

clothes
cocaine
coliseum (or
   colosseum)
colonel
colossal
column
commitment
commodities
compatible
competent
concurrence
condemn
conductor
conduit
conjugal
Connecticut

conscience
consensus
consortium
continuum
corps
correspondence
counterfeit
coup d'état
courtesy
cousin
cryptic
curtain
cylinder
czar

D

database
debugging
deceive
decibel
deductible
defendant
deferred
depot
depreciate
descend
desiccate
desperate

deterrent
develop
diaphragm
dichotomy
dictionary
diesel
digital
dilemma
dinosaur
disappoint
disburse (pay out)
   disperse

discreet
   (cautious)
discrete
   (separate)
disperse (scatter)
   disburse
dissipate
distributor
doubt
dyeing (coloring)
dying (death,
   expiring)

E

ecstasy
eighth
either
elicit (draw forth)
  illicit
embarrass
emphysema
empirical
encyclopedia
endeavor

entrepreneur
envelop (verb)
envelope (noun)
epitome
equipped
equivocal
errata
erroneous
esthetic (or
  aesthetic)

euthanasia
exaggerate
except (other than)
  accept
exhaust
exhibition
exhilarate
existential
exponential
extraterrestrial

F

facsimile
familiar
faze (disturb)
  phase
feasibility
feature
February
fetus
fiduciary

fierce
flourish
fluorescent
fluoridate
foreign
foreseeable
foreword (in a book)
  forward
forfeit

forward (to the
  front)
  foreword
freight
fulfill

G

gallon
gauge
genealogy
generic
geriatrics
gestalt
ghetto

gorilla (primate,
  animal)
  guerrilla
gourmet
governor
graffiti
grammar

grief
grievance
guarantee
guerrilla (revolutionary)
  gorilla
guess
gynecology

H

hallucinogen
harass
Hawaiian
height
heir
hemorrhage

hertz
hiatus
hierarchy
holistic
holocaust
homogeneous

hors d'oeuvre
hydraulic
hygiene
hypocrisy

I

idiosyncrasy
idle (inactive)
idol (image)
illicit (forbidden)
   elicit
impeccable
impetus
impresario
imprimatur

inadvertent
incessant
incumbent
independent
indictment
indispensable
infrared
innocuous
innuendo

inoculate
intermittent
intravenous
iridescent
irrelevant
irresistible
irrevocable
irrigate
island

J

jeopardize
journey

judgment
junta

K

khaki
kibbutz
kilometer

kilowatt
knowledge

L

label
laissez faire
laser
league
legislature
leisure
leukemia

liable
liaison
libel
license
lieu
lieutenant
lightning

likable
likelihood
liquefy
liquor
logarithm

M

maintain
maintenance
malignant
maneuver
manila
margarine
marijuana
marital
marshal
martial
martyr
Massachusetts
massacre

mathematics
mediocre
megabyte
megawatt
memento
menstruation
metaphor
metastasize
microprocessor
migraine
mileage
milieu
miniature

minuscule
minutiae
miscellaneous
mischievous
missile
misspell
mnemonic
modem
monitor
mortgage
mustache

N

naive
necessary
neither

niece
noxious
nozzle

nuance
nuclear

O

occasion
occurrence
odyssey
ombudsman

omniscient
ophthalmologist
overrun

P

panacea
paradigm
parallel
parameter
paraphernalia
parliament
per diem
peremptory
perennial
peripheral
permissible
personnel
perspiration
pharmaceutical

phase (aspect)
  faze
Philippines
phosphorus
physician
placebo
plebiscite
pneumonia
poisonous
pollutant
polymer
porous
posthumous
precede

preferred
prerogative
prevalent
privilege
procedure
proceed
programmer
prophecy (noun)
prophesy (verb)
protein
protocol
pseudonym
publicly
Puerto Rico

Q

quasi
questionnaire
queue

quiche
quorum

R

rapport
rarefy

rebuttal
recede

receipt
receive

reciprocal
recommend
reconnaissance
recuperate
recurrence

referred
rehearsal
relevant
remittance
renaissance

renege
rescind
resistance
rhythm

S

saccharin (noun)
saccharine (adj.)
sacrilegious
satellite
scenario
schedule
scissors
secretary
seizure
separate
sergeant
siege
sight (vision)
   cite
   site
silhouette

similar
simulate
simultaneous
site (location)
   cite
   sight
skeptical
solar
sophomore
spaghetti
stratagem
strategy
stupefy
subpoena (or
   subpena)
subtle

succeed
superintendent
supersede
surprise
surveillance
syllable
synagogue

T

tariff
thief
threshold
tobacco

tongue
toxin
trafficking
trauma

treasurer
trek

U

ubiquitous

unanimous

unnecessary

unprecedented

usage

V

vacuum

vehicle

vengeance

verbatim

veterinarian

vice versa

vicious

villain

W, Y, Z

waiver

weird

wholly

withheld

woolen

yield

zucchini

Plurals of Foreign Words

Singular	Plural
alumnus (masc.)	alumni (masc. or both masc. and fem.)
alumna (fem.)	alumnae (fem.)
axis	axes
crisis	crises
criterion	criteria
datum	data
medium	media *or* mediums
memorandum	memoranda *or* memorandums
nucleus	nuclei
phenomenon	phenomena
stimulus	stimuli
stratum	strata

Anglicized Plurals

Singular	Plural
antenna	antennas *or* antennae (scientific)
appendix	appendixes
cactus	cactuses
formula	formulas
index	indexes *or* indices (scientific)
prospectus	prospectuses

Glossary

Active Voice: The form of the verb to use when the subject performs the action. See Passive Voice and p. 161.

Adjective: Modifies (describes or limits) a noun or pronoun. It may be a single word, phrase, or clause. See p. 5.

> *A <u>good</u> politician is quite as unthinkable as an <u>honest</u> burglar.*—H. L. Mencken

Adverb: Modifies a verb, an adjective, or another adverb. May be a single word, phrase, or clause. See p. 6.

> *The language of advertising...<u>profoundly</u> influences the tongues and pens of children and adults.*—E. B. White

Antecedent: The word, phrase, or clause referred to by a pronoun. In the following example, the pronoun *it* refers to *book;* thus, *book* is the antecedent of *it*.

> *It occurred to me that perhaps writing a <u>book</u> was not as entertaining an activity as signing the contract to write <u>it</u>.*
> —Pete Dexter

Antonym: A word having a meaning opposite to that of another word. *Spicy* is the antonym of *bland*; *ill* is the antonym of *healthy*. See Synonym.

Appositive: A word or phrase that explains the preceding word or phrase. Since appositives are nonrestrictive, they should be surrounded by commas. See p. 63.

> Alfred Nobel, the Swedish chemist and engineer, received a British patent for dynamite in 1867.

Article: The words *a*, *an*, and *the*.

Case: The changes in form made in nouns or pronouns to reflect how they are used in a sentence. For example, the noun *children* is changed to *children's* and the noun *person* is changed to *person's* to show possession. Nouns in English once had many case forms, but the only one used today is the possessive. Pronouns, however, continue to change form to show their relation to the rest of the sentence. The three cases of pronouns are nominative, objective, and possessive. See p. 20.

Clause: A group of words that contains a subject and verb. See p. 12. **Coordinate clauses** have the same grammatical rank and are connected by coordinating conjunctions.

> *The wise make proverbs* and *fools repeat them*.
> —Isaac Disraeli

Dependent clauses (also known as **subordinate clauses**) do not express a complete thought.

> *If you can't annoy somebody*, there is little point in writing.—Kingsley Amis

Independent clauses (also called **principal** or **main clauses**) are complete statements that make sense by themselves.

> *There's no money in poetry*, but then there's no poetry in money either.—Robert Graves

Nonrestrictive clauses could be omitted without changing the meaning; they are separated from the rest of the sentence by commas.

> *Practical men, who believe themselves to be quite exempt from any intellectual influences, are usually the slaves of some defunct economist.*—John Maynard Keynes

Restrictive clauses could not be omitted without changing the meaning of the sentence.

> *The man who walks alone is soon trailed by the F.B.I.*
> —Wright Morris

Cliché: An expression that has lost its freshness by being overused. Examples are *conspicuous by its absence, in the final analysis, add insult to injury,* and *it goes without saying.*

Comma Fault: The error in which a comma is the only punctuation between two independent clauses. Rewrite by replacing the comma with a semicolon or period. See p. 57.

Complement: A word or phrase that completes the meaning of the verb. See p. 11.

> *Great artists need great clients.*—I. M. Pei

> *A human being is nothing but a story with skin around it.*
> —Fred Allen

Compound: Consisting of two or more elements. See p. 116. A **compound adjective,** also known as a unit modifier, consists of two or more adjectives modifying the same noun.

> That <u>swarming, million-footed, tower-masted and sky-soaring</u> citadel that bears the name of the Island of Manhattan.—Thomas Wolfe

A **compound sentence** consists of two or more independent clauses.

> I respect faith, but doubt is what gets you an education.
> —Wilson Mizner

A **compound subject** consists of two or more subjects having the same verb.

> <u>Papa, potatoes, poultry, prunes, and prism</u> are all very good words for the lips; especially prunes and prism.
> —Charles Dickens

A **compound verb** consists of two or more verbs having the same subject.

> The strong winds <u>tore off</u> roofs and <u>blew down</u> power lines.

Conjunction: A single word or group of words that connects other words or groups of words. See p. 6. **Coordinating conjunctions** connect words, phrases, or clauses of equal grammatical rank: *and, but, or, nor, for,* and *so.*

> Some editors are failed writers, <u>but</u> so are most writers.
> —T. S. Eliot

Subordinating conjunctions connect clauses of unequal rank (i.e., an independent and a dependent clause). Examples are *as, as if, because, if, since, that, till, unless, when, where,* and *whether.*

> <u>When</u> I am ready to write a book, I write the ending first.
> —Marcia Davenport

Dangling Modifier: A modifier with an unclear reference. See p. 40.

> <u>Taking the elevator to the fifth floor</u>, the room is easy to find.

Double Negative: Two negative words that cancel each other to create a positive meaning. Such usage is incorrect if it is unintended *(You won't hardly believe this)*, but may be used for its nuances *(The movie was not without its entertaining moments)*. See p. 42.

Gerund: The *-ing* form of a verb that serves as a noun.

> <u>Seeing</u> is <u>believing</u>.

> There must be more to life than <u>having</u> everything.
> —Maurice Sendak

Idiom: A form of expression that, while natural or preferred in a language or region, does not always conform to the rules of grammar or logic. Examples are *rubbing someone the wrong way, taking it easy, stood me in good stead,* and *to make up for.* Though difficult to translate into another language, idioms have a long history of use by good writers.

Infinitive: The form of a verb used with the word *to*.

> *Better to remain silent and be thought a fool than to speak out and remove all doubt.*—Abraham Lincoln

Split infinitives (words inserted between *to* and the verb) have long been an acceptable way to avoid awkward writing.

> Feel free to utterly disregard this formerly steadfast rule.

Interjection: An exclamation such as *Wow!* or *Cool!*

Misplaced Modifier: A modifier that gives a misleading meaning by being incorrectly placed in a sentence. See p. 39.

> The mayor met informally to discuss food prices and the high cost of living with several women.

Mood: Used by a writer to indicate the mode or tone of an action: Is it factual, hypothetical, commanding? See p.15.

Nonrestrictive Elements: Words, phrases, or clauses that add information not essential to the meaning. See Appositive.

> Theobald Tompkins, who has been our neighbor for twenty years, is moving to Arizona next week.

Noun: A word that names a person, place, thing, quality, or act. See p. 4.

Number: Changes made, such as adding an *s*, to reflect whether a word is singular or plural. See p. 14.

Object: The word or phrase that names the thing acted upon by the verb. Objects are complements; they complete the meaning of the verb. See p. 10.

She visited <u>the ancient cathedral</u>.

A **direct object** names the thing acted upon by the verb.

I bought a <u>book</u>.

An **indirect object** receives the direct object.

I bought <u>Aunt Marie</u> a book.

Participle: A form of a verb that has some of the properties of an adjective and some of a verb. Like an adjective, it can modify a noun or pronoun; like a verb, it can take an object. See p. 18.

Success is <u>getting</u> what you want; happiness is <u>wanting</u> what you get.—Charles E. Kettering

In the following examples, the underlined words are participles (verb forms functioning as adjectives):

<u>glowing</u> coals
<u>grayed</u> collars
<u>run-down</u> heels
<u>whipped</u> cream

Parts of Speech: Nouns, pronouns, verbs, adjectives, adverbs, prepositions, conjunctions, and interjections. See p. 3. In the days of *McGuffey's Reader*, students learned the parts of speech with the help of a jingle.

A NOUN's the name of anything;
As, *school* or *garden, hoop* or *swing.*

ADJECTIVES tell the kind of noun;
As, *great, small, pretty, white,* or *brown.*

Instead of nouns the PRONOUNS stand:
Their heads, *your* face, *its* paw, *his* hand.

VERBS tell of something being done:
You *read, count, sing, laugh, jump,* or *run.*

How things are done the ADVERBS tell;
As, *slowly, quickly, ill,* or *well.*

CONJUNCTIONS join the words together;
As, men *and* women, wind *or* weather.

The PREPOSITION stands before
a noun; as, *in* or *through* a door.

The INTERJECTION shows surprise;
As, *Oh!* how pretty! *Ah!* how wise!

Passive Voice: The form of the verb used when the subject is the receiver of the action. See Active Voice and p. 15.

Person: Person denotes the speaker (first person), the person spoken to (second person) or the person or thing spoken about (third person).

Possessive: Showing ownership; also known as the genitive case. See Case.

He is a sheep in <u>sheep's</u> clothing.—Winston Churchill

Predicate: A group of words that makes a statement or asks a question about the subject of a sentence; a predicate is everything in a sentence except the subject. See p. 9. A **simple predicate** consists of a verb.

You <u>can preach</u> a better sermon with your life than with your lips.—Oliver Goldsmith

A **complete predicate** includes verbs, modifiers, objects, and complements.

You <u>can preach a better sermon with your life than with your lips</u>.—Oliver Goldsmith

Prefix: A word element that is attached to the front of a root word and changes the meaning of the root. See Suffix.

<u>dis</u>belief   <u>in</u>attentive

Preposition: A word or group of words that shows the relation between its object and some other word in the sentence. See p. 7.

The playwright needs a producer who will stick <u>by</u> him <u>through</u> thin and thin.—Louis Phillips

Pronoun: A word that represents or stands in for a noun. See p. 5. **Personal pronouns** are *I, you, he, she, it, they* and their inflected forms (*me, my, your, them,* etc.). **Possessive pronouns** indicate ownership.

The book is <u>mine</u>.

Relative pronouns (*who, whom, which, that, what*) join subordinate clauses to their antecedents. In the following sentence, the relative pronoun *who* joins the clause *sang Irish folk songs* with the antecedent *girl*.

The girl <u>who</u> sang Irish folk songs was the star of the show.

Restrictive Elements: Words, phrases, or clauses that are essential to the meaning. See p. 63.

> The joke that gets the most laughs wins the prize.

Run-on: The error of connecting two independent clauses without a conjunction or any punctuation. See p. 56.

Sentence: A group of words that contains at least one subject and predicate and expresses a complete thought. See p. 12. A **simple sentence** consists of subject and predicate (in other words, an independent clause).

> *My speed depends on the state of my bank account.*
> —Mickey Spillane

> *Just sit down at the typewriter and open a vein.*—Red Smith

A **compound sentence** consists of two or more independent clauses.

> *Life is a shipwreck, but we must not forget to sing in the lifeboats.*—Voltaire

A **complex sentence** consists of one independent clause and one or more dependent (subordinate) clauses; in the following example, the independent clause is underlined.

> *New York is the only city in the world where you can be deliberately run down on the sidewalk by a pedestrian.*
> —Russell Baker

Subject: The part of a sentence about which something is said. See p. 9.

> Time flies.

You can identify the subject by asking *what* or *who*; your answer is the subject. (What flies? Time flies.)

> *Some <u>people</u> think <u>they</u> are worth a lot of money because <u>they</u> have it.*—Edmund Fuller

Subordinate Clause: See Clause, Dependent.

Suffix: A word element added to the end of a root or stem word and serving to make a new word or an inflected form of the word. Thus, *-ness* and *-ren* added to *gentle* and *child* create the new word *gentleness* and the inflected word *children*. Other examples of suffixes are mother*hood*, depend*able*, arrange*ment*, end*ed*, and walk*ing*. See Prefix.

Synonym: A word having a meaning identical with or very similar to that of another word. *Shout* is a synonym for *yell*; *likely* is a synonym for *probable*. See Antonym.

Tense: Tells when an action takes place (present, future, past). See p. 15.

Unit Modifier: See Compound Adjective.

Verb: A word that expresses action, being, or occurrence. See pp. 4 and 14.

> Time <u>flies</u>.

Voice: See Active Voice, Passive Voice.

Bibliography

Alred, Gerald J., Charles T. Brusaw, and Walter E. Olim. *The Business Writer's Handbook*, 6th ed. New York: Bedford/St. Martin's Press, 2000.

——. *The Handbook of Technical Writing*, 6th ed. New York: Bedford/St. Martin's Press, 2000.

Amis, Kingsley. *The King's English: A Guide to Modern Usage*. New York: St. Martin's Press, 1999.

Bates, Jefferson D. *Writing with Precision: How to Write so that You Cannot Possibly Be Misunderstood*. New York: Penguin Books, 2000.

Bernstein, Theodore. *The Careful Writer: A Modern Guide to English Usage*. Rockland, ME: Free Press, 1995.

Boston, Bruce O., ed. *STET! Tricks of the Trade for Writers and Editors*. Alexandria, VA: EEI Press, 1995.

Brians, Paul. *The Great Grammar Challenge*. Alexandria, VA: EEI Press, 1998.

Chapman, Robert L., ed. *Roget's International Thesaurus*, 5th ed. New York: HarperCollins, 1992.

EEI Communications Staff. *STET Again! More Tricks of the Trade for Publications People*. Alexandria, VA: EEI Press, 1996.

Follett, Wilson. *Modern American Usage: A Guide*. New York: Hill & Wang, 1998.

Fowler, H. W. *A Dictionary of Modern English Usage*, 2nd rev. ed. New York and Oxford, England: Oxford University Press, 1983.

Garner, Bryan A. *The Oxford Dictionary of American Usage and Style*. New York: Berkley Books, 2000.

Gibaldi, Joseph. *MLA Handbook for Writers of Research Papers*, 5th ed. New York: Modern Language Assn. of America, 1999.

Gorrell, Donna. *A Writer's Handbook, from A to Z*, 2nd ed. Needham Heights, MA: Allyn & Bacon, 1997.

Hacker, Diana. *A Pocket Style Manual*, 3rd ed. New York: Bedford/St. Martin's Press, 2000.

Hackos, Joann T., and Dawn M. Stevens. *Standards for Online Communications*. New York: John Wiley & Sons, 1997.

Hale, Constance, ed. *Wired Style: Principles of English Usage in the Digital Age*, rev. ed. New York: Broadway Books, 2000.

Harrison, Gwen. *Vocabulary Dynamics*. New York: Warner Books, 1992.

James, Ewart. *NTC's Dictionary of British Slang and Colloquial Expressions*. Lincolnwood, IL: NTC/Contemporary Publishing Company, 1997.

Lederer, Richard, and Richard Dowis. *Sleeping Dogs Don't Lay*. New York: St. Martin's Press, 1999.

Lovinger, Paul W. *The Penguin Dictionary of American English Usage and Style*. New York: Penguin Reference, 2000.

Manhard, Stephen J. *The Goof Proofer/How to Avoid the 41 Most Embarrassing Errors in Your Speaking and Writing*. New York: Macmillan Publishing Co., 1998.

McClanahan, Rebecca. *Word Painting: A Guide to Writing More Descriptively*. Cincinnati, OH: Writer's Digest Books, 1999.

Morris, William, and Mary Morris. *Harper Dictionary of Contemporary Usage*. New York: Harper & Row, 1985.

Pavlicin, Karen, and Christy Lyon. *Online Style Guide: Terms, Usage and Tips*. St. Paul, MN: Elva Resa Publishing, 1998.

Plotnik, Arthur. *The Elements of Expression: Putting Thoughts into Words*. New York: Macmillan Publishing Co., 2000.

Podheiser, Mary Elizabeth. *Painless Spelling*. New York: Barron's, 1998.

Rico, Gabriele. *Writing the Natural Way*, rev. ed. New York: Jeremy P. Tarcher, 2000.

Ross-Larson, Bruce. *The Effective Writing Series: (1) Stunning Sentences, (2) Riveting Reports, (3) Powerful Paragraphs*. New York: W. W. Norton, 1999.

Sammons, Martha C. *The Internet Writer's Handbook*. Needham Heights, MA: Allyn & Bacon, 1999.

Shaw, Harry. *Errors in English and Ways to Correct Them*. New York: HarperCollins, 1993.

Spears, Richard A. *NTC's American Idioms Dictionary*. Lincolnwood, IL: NTC/Contemporary Publishing Company, 1991.

Strunk, William, and E. B. White. *The Elements of Style*, 4th ed. Needham Heights, MA: Allyn and Bacon, 2000.

Sun Technical Publications. *Read Me First: A Style Guide for the Computer Industry*. Palo Alto, CA: Sun Microsystems Press, 1996.

Sutcliffe, Andrea J., ed. *The New York Public Library Writer's Guide to Style and Usage*. New York: HarperCollins, 1994.

Tarshis, Barry. *Grammar for Smart People: Your User-Friendly Guide to Speaking and Writing Better English*. New York: Pocket Books, 1993.

Turabian, Kate L. *A Manual for Writers of Term Papers, Theses, and Dissertations*, 6th ed. Chicago: University of Chicago Press, 1996.

University of Chicago Press. *The Chicago Manual of Style*, 14th ed. Chicago: University of Chicago Press, 1993.

United States Government Printing Office. *Style Manual*, rev. ed. Washington, DC: Government Printing Office, 2000.

Venolia, Jan. *Kids Write Right! What You Need to Be a Writing Powerhouse*. Berkeley, CA: Tricycle Press, 2000.

———. *Rewrite Right! Your Guide to Perfectly Polished Prose*. Berkeley, CA: Ten Speed Press, 2000.

———. *Better Letters: A Handbook of Business and Personal Correspondence*. Berkeley, CA: Ten Speed Press, 1995.

Vitanza, Victor J. *Writing for the World Wide Web*. Needham Heights, MA: Allyn & Bacon, 1997.

Walker, Janice R., and Todd W. Taylor. *The Columbia Guide to Online Styling*. New York: Columbia University Press, 1998.

Walsh, Bill. *Lapsing into a Comma: A Curmudgeon's Guide to the Many Things that Can Go Wrong in Print—and How to Avoid Them*. Chicago: Contemporary Books, 2000.

Wittels, Harriet, and Joan Greisman. *A Handbook of Commonly Misspelled Words*. New York: Grosset & Dunlap, 2000.

Zinsser, William K. *On Writing Well*, 6th ed. New York: HarperCollins, 1998.

Web Sites

The amount of information on the Internet can be daunting, and it sometimes comes in commercial packages primarily designed to sell books and services. Nonetheless, if you are selective in your searches, you will find much to help you.

Although I've explored each of the sites listed below, new ones appear and old ones disappear in the fluid world of the Internet, so I make no claims for completeness or accuracy. But even if a site is no longer available, along the way you may encounter just what you need. Enjoy the process!

Writing Guides

These sites, in addition to presenting useful information about writing (punctuation, grammar, usage) have links to additional sites of possible interest. When looking for help with a particular writing problem, start with one of these.

http://www.wsu.edu/~brians/

Paul Brians of Washington State University created and maintains this site with flair. In addition to the serious stuff, he includes Mr. Gradgrind's answers to rhetorical questions, such as "What is so rare as a day in June," and "Who's afraid of Virginia Woolf."

http://andromeda.rutgers.edu/~jlynch/writing/

Jack Lynch of Rutgers University has packed this site with information. Click on "Guide to Grammar & Style" to explore its many facets. And, should you want to know anything about a moose, click on "Moose Resources." Never let it be said that an English professor doesn't have a sense of humor.

http://www.robinsnest.com

Created and maintained by Robin Nobles, an author and teacher, this site has links to the above two sites, as well as many others of interest to writers.

http://www.theslot.com/

This idiosyncratic site is the work of Bill Walsh of the *Washington Post*. In segments with titles like Carets & Sticks, and Sharp Points, Walsh presents views on writing of special interest to journalists.

http://ccc.commnet.edu/grammar

Charles Darling of Capital Community College maintains this site, which presents half a dozen menus to choose from (e.g., Word & Sentence Level, Ask Grammar, Quizzes, and Index). Includes an extensive list of Notorious Confusables.

http://www.edufind.com/english/grammar/

The Online English Grammar, created by Anthony Hughes, provides free online English grammar resources.

Information About the Web and the Internet

http://www.northernwebs.com/bc

Beginners' Central, where you will find basic information about downloading, advanced search techniques, and so on, plus Myths of the Internet and a glossary.

http://www.about-the-web.com

Topics include avoiding scams, Great Web Sites, glossary, and a free newsletter, "What's New about the Web."

http://www.learnthenet.com/english

Basic information for Web novices.

http://www.help.com

Includes the offer of a free Tweak Freak Newsletter to "show you how to squeeze every last drop of performance out of your system."

http://www.hansenmedia.com

"Your Digital Media Reference Source."

Dictionaries and Glossaries

http://www.yourdictionary.com

Includes definitions and links to online resources, but not as rich a resource as a dictionary in print form.

http://www.acronymfinder.com
Decodes acronyms for you.

http://www.csgnetwork.com/glossary.html
Computer, telephony, and electronics glossary.

http://www.hotwired.lycos.com/webmonkey/guides
Glossary of Internet terms, such as *HTML* and *ethernet,* as well as abbreviations like nrn (no reply necessary) and rotfl (rolling on the floor laughing).

Reference Sites/Research Tools

http://writetools.com/
"A one-stop reference center for anyone who writes, edits, or checks facts." Sources include everything from Almanacs to Zip Codes.

http://www.powerreporting.com/
"Free research tools for journalists" include grammar and style guides.

http://www.thescratchingpost.com/wordsmithshop/writing.html
Extensive information about writing for the World Wide Web.

http://www.sharpwriter.com/
Includes dictionaries, thesauruses, grammar and punctuation guides, quotations (one of the more commercial sites).

Plain Language Sites

The following two sites advocate plain language in writing (hear, hear!).

http://www.plainlanguage.gov

Includes a PDF version of "Writing User-Friendly Documents" and offers an Adobe Acrobat Reader to view this PDF version. Look for "Plain English Handbook."

http://www.adler.demon.co.uk/clarity.htm

This site is maintained by Clarity, a "worldwide lawyers' group campaigning for plain legal language."

All of the Above

www.verbivore.com

Well, maybe not quite "all," but author Richard Lederer has come close to creating an omnipurpose language Web site. A click on "Language Links on the Internet" provides a host of choices: Etymology, Grammar & Usage, Language Columns (e.g., Grammar Lady, Word for Word), Puns, Word Games, Vocabulary Development, Dictionaries; "Other Language Reference Links" leads to yet another layer of word stuff (e.g., slang, clichés, new words, American vs. English usage). It also includes excerpts from Lederer's books and information about his lecture tours.

Index

Rewrite
Right!

> Mend your speech a little,
> lest it mar your fortune.—*Shakespeare*
>
> Mend your writing, too.
> —*Jan Venolia*

Contents

1 Why Rewrite?

> I have rewritten—often several times—
> every word I have ever published.
> My pencils outlast their erasers.
> —*Vladimir Nabokov*

As a writer or editor today, you have a lot more at your disposal than pencils and erasers.

- Word-processing software simplifies writing and revising, from note-taking and first drafts to final copy.

- The Internet is a reference library at your fingertips.

- E-mail makes keeping in touch with colleagues, friends, and family a snap and eases the interaction among authors, editors, peer reviewers, project managers, and production staff.

These powerful tools *help you do it,* but a solid foundation in the principles of revising tells you *what needs to be done.*

Rewrite Right! is for people who must write at work or in school and for freelance writers struggling to make sales. Editing is improving something written—making it easier to follow, snappier, more interesting. Knowing how to edit means

1

knowing what good writing is in the first place. And good writing comes from knowing how to revise, how to tug on words and adjust them until they say what you want them to say. In other words, writing and editing are facets of the same subject: doing a good job of putting ideas into words.

Have advances in telecommunications reduced the need for good writing? Not at all. The medium may change, but the language still needs to be well crafted. People who used to step down the hall to brainstorm with a colleague now sit down at a keyboard and whip out a message on e-mail.

E-mail has many advantages. It's convenient, fast, cheap, and less intrusive than a phone call; it provides a paper trail and is easily distributed to a large number of people. It allows an increasing number of people to work from their homes.

But the very ease of e-mail can be a hazard. Many people have developed an e-mail style that's breezy and informal; they pay less attention to spelling and grammar than they would in a standard letter. Should they care about good writing? You bet! E-mail recipients shouldn't have to puzzle their way through a message riddled with misspelled or omitted words and confusing references. Don't let the informality of e-mail fool you into thinking sloppiness is okay. Spontaneity is fine; sloppiness can be dangerous in any communication.

Muddled instructions create confusion. Costly research is repeated because results are buried in an obscure, two-pound report. Boring writing is tossed aside unread. Slipshod writing breeds distrust, prompting readers to wonder if language is the writer's only area of incompetence.

At the other end of the spectrum, good writing gets things done. Its crisp, clear style requires less of the reader's time. Good writing lowers administrative expenses, lightens workloads, and suggests the writer is competent in other areas as well.

Yet when it comes to writing, many capable people falter. They may be experts at marketing or high-energy physics, but ask them to write it up, and they rely on worn-out expressions and stilted prose.

As a consulting editor, I've learned where most people need help. My first two books, *Write Right!* and *Better Letters*, provide simple advice.

Rewrite Right! is for those who want more. It describes two levels of editing: (1) to improve style and content, and (2) to correct language.

Rewrite Right! includes a variety of reference materials: lists of accepted abbreviations, hackneyed expressions, common redundancies, and irregular plurals. It suggests ways to make a document look better and explores sophisticated tools available to today's writers and editors. A glossary provides definitions of unfamiliar terms.

I hope *Rewrite Right!* helps you learn not only to write and rewrite well, but to enjoy doing it.

2 Writing and Editing in the 21st Century

> Don't be afraid to seize whatever you have written and cut it to ribbons. It can always be restored to its original condition in the morning.—*E. B. White*
>
> Especially if you have the right software.
> —*Jan Venolia*

Today's sophisticated software puts a dazzling variety of tools at your fingertips. Use them in the early stages of writing to take notes, outline, and create rough drafts. Use them in the revising process to explore various formats, insert and delete text, and rearrange paragraphs or whole sections. Use them in the final stages to add graphics and captions, introduce desktop publishing touches (e.g., borders, shading, drop caps), and print final, camera-ready copies.

The Internet as Writing Resource

The Internet is a rich source of information about writing and revising. There you will find the principles of good writing, lists of common errors, interactive quizzes, online dictionaries, guidelines for gender-fair writing, and compilations of web-based writing centers.

But you need to exercise caution, because some of the information is inaccurate or outdated. For example, William Strunk's classic, *The Elements of Style,* is online in the original 1918 edition, not the modern version edited by E. B. White.

The very quantity of information is daunting. Arm yourself with a clear objective for your web searches, so you will be able to screen out extraneous material and reap the benefits of having the world at your fingertips.

Outlining

An outline helps break through the intimidating nature of a blank page; you feel that you've begun and can see a path to the end. An outline forces you to think about which are the more important topics, the ones to be emphasized and buttressed with supporting detail.

If you choose a standard outline format (topic, subtopic, sub-subtopic), your computer will simplify the process. You can:

- Add topics and subtopics

- Change a subtopic to a topic and rearrange topics as your outline evolves

- Insert a block of text

- Display or print an outline by topic level or in its entirety

If you prefer a free-form, handwritten outline, with circles and spokes or tree trunks with branches, your activity is more like brainstorming. That's all right! Dump your ideas on the page and then look for ways to tie them together.

But whether you use a computer, index cards, flip charts and marking pens, or lined yellow pads, an outline is a powerful tool. By boiling down the essence of your writing into just a few words, an outline helps you discover imbalances, discontinuities, or omissions. It tells you if you've delivered on the promise implied by your headings. It ferrets out irrelevant material. Take the time at the outset to develop an outline—it will pay big dividends.

Writing and Revising

Word processors have blurred the distinction between writing and editing. The once sharply defined steps of writing, analyzing, and revising are now integrated into a more smoothly flowing whole. You revise as you write, and write as you revise. You can be more daring and experimental knowing that you can easily make changes.

Early on, establish a suitable format for your document. Determine the margins and spacing and then either create your own format or choose a prepackaged style that matches your needs. Left justification of margins (in which the text is evenly lined up at the left margin) is the norm, but with the click of a mouse you can choose full justification (text evenly lined up at both left and right margins). You have a wide variety of type fonts and sizes to choose from, and individual words can be *italicized*, <u>underlined</u>, or set in **boldface.** Footnotes[1], subscripts (H_2O), and superscripts (10^{-27}) are easy to add.

You also have a variety of ways to modify text. You can delete individual words, lines, paragraphs—whole chunks of text. You can move them to a better spot, using Cut and Paste. Did you misspell a name? Correct it throughout the document with Find and Replace. Need to remove double spaces following periods? Find and Replace is your ally.

If you use certain paragraphs repeatedly, as in resumés, proposals, or promotional documents, you can store such boilerplate (for example, in AutoText) and drop it in where you need it.

When I can't decide between alternative wordings, I type the choices I'm considering in brackets. Later, as I edit the document, I delete the rejected alternative with a click.

Software tutorials cover the basics of writing fiction, nonfiction, and drama. Some programs use a question-and-answer format to help you plug holes in a plot or strengthen weak characters. Programs for screenwriters simplify the formatting of dialogue by eliminating repetitious typing of names.

Whether it's relatively unsophisticated or state-of-the-art, your word processor is much more than a fancy typewriter.

---

[1]See? It's a snap.

Checking Spelling and Grammar

A spell-checker is a valuable tool for catching misspelled or unintentionally doubled words. But be aware of its limitations.

Spell-checked documents may still include incorrect words. A spell-checker assumes a correctly spelled word is the right word. If you write *thier house*, the spell-checker will point out your error. But if you write *there house*, your mistake will go unnoticed.

I laughed out loud recently when I read of someone reaching "the first wrung of the ladder." Wrong rung! Most of us don't want to be laughed at, so careful proofing with the frequent use of a dictionary is still necessary. (See Chapter 8 for rules to help you become a better speller.)

A spell-checker also assumes any word it doesn't recognize is misspelled, so it flags many correct words, including names, acronyms, compound words, and hyphenated words. You can reduce this nuisance by adding frequently used proper names or acronyms to the spell-checker's vocabulary.

Grammar-checkers are even more limited. They sometimes incorrectly flag text, on the one hand, and overlook obvious errors on the other. Here are some of the "errors" a grammar-checker found in a draft of this book.

- It suggested that "paper and pencil are" should be changed to "paper and pencil is." Evidently its operating rules for agreement of subject and verb don't include compound subjects.

- It wanted me to change "most of whom write poorly" to "most of who write poorly." That's just plain wrong. (See p. 122 for help with *who* and *whom*—especially if you are a programmer who writes software programs for grammar-checkers!)

- It failed to catch the incorrect apostrophe in "writer's and editors agree…."

A grammar-checker won't find ambiguous words or incomplete sentences. It won't tell you which words to capitalize other than "I" and the first word of a sentence. It doesn't force you to think about your audience or the logic behind your presentation. It doesn't catch faulty references or misplaced modifiers.

Is a grammar-checker worth turning on? I find it useful in determining readability. A grammar-checker lists the number of sentences, number of words, average sentence length, and average word length. It counts the words in the shortest and longest sentences and identifies both. It can help you find overworked words by listing them according to the number of times they appear. Some programs will calculate the school-grade level needed to read a document.

Tracking Revisions

The ability to track revisions has removed one of the hazards of editing online. Previously, those golden words you thought you could improve upon—and then changed your mind—might have disappeared entirely. Today's word-processing software allows you to highlight and keep track of changes made in the text, even when more than one person is making the changes.

Here are a few features commonly available:

- New material is underlined and added to the text; deletions remain but are crossed out. This allows you to see exactly what has been added and deleted.

- Changes made by different individuals appear in different colors; the identity of the individual can be revealed by clicking on a revision.

- Changes can be highlighted on the screen only or on both the screen and the printed document. The original can be compared with edited versions, side by side on the screen. Changes can be accepted or rejected—repeatedly—if you later change your mind.

- Non-printing notes or comments (for on-screen viewing) can be inserted; a block of text can be highlighted for later revision.

Editing via E-Mail

E-mail is a great timesaver when you need to circulate drafts of documents among authors, editors, and project managers who aren't just down the hall from each other. What used to take days by mail and express delivery services can now be done in minutes.

To be sure, zapping text from one spot to another introduces new hazards. You must deal with the possibility of viruses and of PC-Mac file incompatibility. If you are alert to the need to find and remove garbage resulting from attachment errors (for example, an em-dash appears as the word "emdash" instead of the dash itself), you will have overcome the main problem in sending manuscripts via e-mail.

You also need to be sure that everyone in the process is operating under the same guidelines. This may mean writing your own instructions (everything from a one-page memo to a small booklet, depending on the complexity of the project). Everyone needs to know how to flag alterations, queries, and comments within a document, and how to control various versions (original, revised, and final). But once you've established

EDITING BY E-MAIL

1. Author submits text to Project Manager/Editor (PM/E) via e-mail. Anyone whose e-mail programs resist attachments can cut-and-paste the text into the body of the e-mail message.

2. PM/E checks for viruses, and if necessary, converts the files into the in-house word-processing software. PM/E also cleans up any formatting garbage that may have been introduced in the transmission; PM/E creates a project file and forwards copies of the draft to the editor.

3. Editor makes corrections in boldface; any queries are bracketed with an agreed-upon symbol such as a double plus sign, to avoid being confused with the text. The edited copy becomes the master copy, which is e-mailed back to the author using cut-and-paste to avoid introducing garbage (author is warned that no formatting will be seen in this version).

4. Author responds to queries and suggested changes right in the document, again using an agreed-upon symbol to set off any changes made. The resulting version is given a new file name to differentiate it from the original document.

5. PM/E puts both master copy and final draft submitted by author on screen, searches for the symbol, and then copies and pastes the alterations in the final draft into the master copy. PM/E sends master copy to production/layout and then on to proofreader.

6. PM/E sends paper copy to author for final check.

those procedures in your instructions, you'll find e-mail to be indispensable.

With such procedures in place, you have the desired, uniform results in a fraction of the time needed for sending hard copies around. In fact, you will probably wonder how you ever managed without e-mail.

Can you rely on software to do the whole editing job? No. In fact, the attractive appearance of pages created with state-of-the-art gadgetry may mask underlying flaws. The essential ingredients are still good judgment and your knowledge of writing fundamentals.

3 Getting Started

> No passion in the world is equal to the passion to alter someone else's draft.
> —H. G. Wells
>
> Unless it's the resistance to sitting down and editing your own.—Jan Venolia

The key to good rewriting is dividing the job into two parts: first-level editing, in which you tackle the substance of the writing (organization, content, style), and second-level editing, in which you correct the language (punctuation, grammar, mechanics). Second-level editing is also known as copyediting.

Two-Level Editing

When you wear both first- and second-level hats, wear only one hat at a time. Efficiency in editing comes not from a single, all-purpose reading, but from several readings, each with a different focus.

Look first at content and style. It's easier to detect abrupt transitions between paragraphs or poorly supported arguments in the first reading. Flag other problems for a later reading—and keep moving. You don't want to bog down in minor corrections when you're looking for flaws of organization and logic.

And you don't want to waste time punctuating a sentence that you later delete.

Look for specific types of problems in separate readings. Do verbs flip between past and present tense without reason? You can catch such disconcerting lapses more easily if you skim once looking only at verbs. Are the captions of illustrations and tables parallel in form? If you devote one reading to captions, you are more likely to notice inconsistencies.

Editing Someone Else's Writing

You face certain challenges when editing someone else's writing. It's easier to catch places where a reader might stumble; it's harder to deal with prickly egos. Making all the changes you think necessary while remaining on good terms with the author requires tact. Keep in mind that the author has already invested a lot of time, and your suggestions will probably call for an additional investment.

Avoid being confrontational: "That paragraph makes no sense," or "You're going to make us miss our deadline." Instead, look for ways to unruffle feathers: "I understand how you feel," "I'll take care of it," "Yes." Find ways to help the author convey ideas more forcefully.

Make sure what kind and amount of editing is desired. If you are expected to use only a light touch, look for errors in spelling and punctuation. Check for consistency of format, captions, treatment of acronyms, capitalization, compound words, and numbers. Such details contribute to smooth, orderly writing. You should also suggest substitutes for the author's pet words and reposition any misplaced modifiers.

On the other hand, if you are expected to review material for technical accuracy or readability, you haven't helped much if all you did was add commas or hyphenate compound words. Assume that something you find confusing or jarring will probably confuse or jar another reader, too. Be specific in letting the author know the nature of the problem by rewriting the troublesome parts.

Rein in overwritten prose, and point out areas where too much has been left out. Inject vigor where the writing is lifeless, and cool the rhetoric if the author is carried away with cleverness. But don't insinuate your personality into the writing, making it a crazy quilt of different styles. Above all, don't change an author's meaning. Handled skillfully, the author-editor synergy produces better writing than either individual could create alone.

Editing Your Own Writing

Being your own editor presents different challenges. It's hard to develop the distance needed for evaluating what you've written. Take a break before revising to help shift your perceptions from writer to reader. See the document with fresh eyes, as if for the first time.

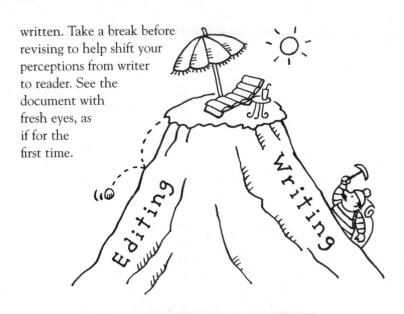

> Good writing is good manners. You can both please and help your public only when you learn how to be the first victim of your writing, how to anticipate a reader's difficulties, and to hear yourself as others hear you.—*Ritchie R. Ward*

An editing checklist is a good way to begin. It asks questions to get you started and confirms that you haven't overlooked anything important.

The checklist on pp. 19–22 serves a dual purpose: (1) It reviews the fundamentals of writing and revising; (2) it acquaints you with the contents of this book.

AN EDITING CHECKLIST

First-Level Editing: To Improve Writing
   Audience:
— Is the writing directed to a specific reader or type of reader?
— Does the writing match what is known about the audience?
— Does the approach take the reader's level of knowledge into account?
   • For a lay audience, are terms defined? Examples provided?
   • For an audience of experts, are enough supporting facts presented?
   • Are conclusions backed up by evidence?
— Do examples help the reader understand?
— Are answers provided for the questions readers are most likely to ask?
— Does the writing have the right tone, the right amount of formality or informality?
— Is the writing bias-free?
   • Have you used slanted words, inappropriate labels, or stereotypes?
   • Have you given parallel treatment in matters of sex, race, age, and ability?
     See *Write to Your Audience*, p. 29.

   Logic:
— Are the ideas clear?
— Was there a plan? Was it followed?
— Is the information coherent?
— Is it presented according to a logical scheme?
     See *Have a Plan*, p. 37.

Interest:

— Does the title enlighten and intrigue?
— Are headings helpful?
— Does the beginning make the reader want to read on?
— Are important points emphasized?
— Is there variety in kinds of sentences, in sentence lengths, in paragraph lengths?
— Does the ending provide a sense of completion?

> See *Grab Their Attention*, p. 43.

Clarity:

— Are any words or sentences ambiguous?
— Are antecedents clear? (Will readers understand what words like *it* and *this* refer to?)
— Are words specific rather than vague?
— Do you signal what's coming by such words as *but* or *therefore*?
— Have unintentional double negatives slipped in?

> See *Make It Clear*, p. 53.

Brevity, Conciseness:

— Are there too many words?
— Are there redundancies?

> See *Trim the Lard*, p. 64.

Usage:

— Do the words convey the desired meaning?
— Are singular and plural words used correctly?

> See *Know Your Words*, p. 69.

— Are there overworked expressions?

> See *Cut Clichés and Hackneyed Expressions*, p. 73.

— Do you use the active voice wherever possible?

— Have you avoided lifeless verbs (*to be, exist, occur*)?
— Are words unnecessarily hedged with qualifiers (*almost, somewhat, very, little*)?
See *Speak Out*, p. 76.
— Does gobbledygook create a verbal smokescreen?
See *Jettison Jargon*, p. 80.
— Do the words create the right kind of picture?
— Are metaphors effective?
See *Evoke Images*, p. 83.
— Are small words like *a, an,* and *the* used correctly?
— Are contractions used correctly (especially *it's* and *there's*)?
See *Watch Small Words*, p. 85.

Second-Level Editing: To Correct Language
Punctuation:
— Do punctuation marks help readers grasp the meaning?
— Is there any surplus punctuation?
See *Punctuation*, p. 89.

Grammar:
— Do subjects and verbs agree?
— Do pronouns and antecedents agree?
See *Agreement*, p. 114.
— Are pronouns in their correct case (*who* or *whom, I, me,* or *myself*)?
— Do pronouns refer clearly to their antecedents?
See *Pronouns*, p. 121.
— Did you remove dangling and misplaced modifiers?
See *Adjectives and Adverbs*, p. 125.
— Are the tense and mood of verbs consistent?
See *Verbs*, p. 128.

— Are related parts of sentences or headings parallel in form?

See *Parallel Structure*, p. 132.

— Are sentences complete (i.e., no fragments)?
— Are there any run-ons?

See *No-Fault Sentences*, p. 132.

Mechanics:

— Are abbreviations kept to a minimum? Are they used correctly?

See *Abbreviations*, p. 135.

— Is capitalization correct and consistent?

See *Capitalization*, p. 140.

— Are numbers below 10 spelled out? Are numbers of 10 and above written as figures?

See *Numbers*, p. 149.

— Are words correctly spelled?
— Is the treatment of compounds consistent (as one word, two words, or hyphenated)?

See *Spelling*, p. 152.

— If your writing includes quoted material, have the quotations been presented correctly?

See *Quotations*, p. 161.

— Is hyphenation at the right margin minimized?
— Are words divided correctly?

See *Word Division*, p. 162.

— Are there any gaps in page numbering?
— Are all tables and figures included and numbered correctly?
— Does the table of contents match the text?

See *Document Integrity*, p. 165.

— Is the layout (format) attractive?
— Is it easy to read?

See *Document Appearance*, p. 166.

Style Sheet

As you edit, use a style sheet to keep track of decisions you make about spelling (*esthetic* or *aesthetic*), capitalization (*Federal* or *federal*), and the treatment of compound words (*E-Mail, e-mail, email*). Style sheets are useful if you are the only editor, essential if two or more people are editing the same material.

To make a style sheet, divide a blank page into boxes. Put a few letters of the alphabet at the top of each box. Reserve a box or two for acronyms and numbers. When you come to a place in the manuscript where a style choice such as spelling or capitalization has been made, write in the appropriate box the term and page number where the word first appears. Thus, *subpoena* would go in the R, S, T, U, V box to show its spelling. *Low-grade infection* would go in the I, J, K, L, M box to show the hyphenation. Each time you encounter such a term, refer to the style sheet to see how you treated it before.

The principle is the same when you create a style sheet with your word processor. Instead of creating boxes, put the groups of letters flush with the left margin; as you come to an example in the text of a decision made, type the word or phrase under the appropriate letter.

Proofreading

Proofreading is the last step in the writer's quality-assurance program. It consists of comparing the "proof" (the printed pages produced by the typist or typesetter) with the author's final draft. The objective is to confirm that editing changes have actually been made and to catch any new typos or errors that previously escaped notice.

STYLE SHEET

A B C D

dialogue	53
bi-lingual	106
bodacious	12
Breathalyzer	46
ad hominem	73

E F G H

Federalism	72, 79
eminence grise	51
halftone	43
freelance	103-5, 110
European Common Market	79

I J K L M

middle-class junkies	66
machismo	67
lowercase	21, 23, 85

N O P Q

question-begging generalization	25
the Pentagon	89
Op-Ed page	66
palimony	67, 69

R S T U V

under way	153
renege	94
right-to-die movement	123
uppercase	21, 23, 86

W X Y Z

white-collar crime	15
win-win situation	12
X-rated films	34

NUMBERS

the 20's	12

ACRONYMS, ABBREVIATIONS

OPEC	34-7
IRA	59

Incomplete revision is an increasingly common cause of proof-reading error. A new wording is inserted, but remnants of the previous wording remain. For example, if you change "It can easily be distributed..." to "It is easily distributed..." but fail to remove one of the no-longer-needed words, the sentence will read, "It is easily be distributed...."

Authors should be the first to proofread their work. But since they often don't see their own mistakes, it's smart to have another person proofread as well. Important documents should be proofread by two people working together. One person reads aloud from the proof while the other follows along with the author's final draft. The reader should speak clearly and call out beginnings of paragraphs, italics, capitalization, and all punctuation marks.

If only one proofreader is a good speller, have that person be the one reading the proof. Presumably spell-checkers will have caught all the *misspelled* words by this stage, but there may well be *wrong* words (*site* instead of *cite*, for example). It's up to the proofreader to know if it's the right word.

If you don't have a proofreading partner, use two rulers to track the lines of text being compared. Keep the following questions in mind:

- Have any words or lines been left out?

- Have all deleted letters or words actually been removed?

- Have revisions created unacceptable breaks at the end of a line or page?

- Have any typos slipped in?

When you have made one correction in a sentence, re-read the entire sentence. In concentrating on the first error, you may have missed a later one.

> Typos that produce legitimate words are hard to catch and sometimes unintentionally funny. Here are some of my favorites—all of which would be missed by a spell-checker.
>
> Look for prescription drugs on which the patients have expired.
>
> The militia went into the countryside, fathering troops.
>
> The great steal of the State of New Jersey...
>
> The copulation statistics reveal a high level of mobility.

Make your corrections bold and clear. On double-spaced type-written pages, you can enter minor corrections between lines as long as the corrections are legible and understandable. On single-spaced or typeset material, place corrections in the margins, with a mark ($\wedge$) to indicate where to insert the change. If a change doesn't fit in the margin or between the lines, put it on a slip of paper and attach the paper, properly identified, to the page to be changed. Use sticky notes to remind yourself to verify a statistic or check a reference.

Run a "delete line" ($\swarrow$) through letters, words, or phrases to be removed. Run a diagonal line through a capital letter you want to make lowercase.

If you change your mind about something you've crossed out, write "stet" in the margin. If you want to restore only part of the crossed-out material, put a dot under each letter you want retained.

If you add punctuation marks directly in the text instead of in the margin, mark them so they won't be overlooked. Circle any periods ⊙ or hyphens ⊖ ; put carets above commas ⌄ and below quotation marks ⌄⌄ , apostrophes ⌄ , and footnote numbers ⌄ .

Proofreader's marks are an efficient shorthand; they originated in the printing industry but have been widely adopted. If you use these marks, be sure the person typing the corrected draft

PROOFREADER'S MARKS

_ℓ_ delete	(tr) transpose
⌒ close up space	
# insert space	[move left
ê/or insert letter punctuation word	] move right
cap uppercase	] center [
_l.c._ lowercase	(ital) set in <u>italic</u>
stet do not make correction	(bf) set in boldface
¶ Begin paragraph.	(sp) spell out
_no_ ¶ no new paragraph	

understands their meaning. A photocopy of these marks should do the trick.

(bf)] ᴧMARKED-UP MANUSCRIPT [

An American, instead of going in a leisure hour
to dance merrily at some place of public resort as
the fellows of his calling continue to do
throughout the greater part of europe, shuts (cap)
home himself up at to drink.

no¶/(sp) He thus enjoys (2) pleasures; he can go on thinking (tr)
of his business, and he can get drunk decently
drunk by his own fireside. . . . ¶In America I saw
the freest and most enlightened men, placed in the
happiest circumstances which the world affords.
[Yet] it seemed to me as if a cloud habitually hung
upon their brow, and I thought them serious and #
almost sad even in their pleasures . . . , forever
brooding over advantages they do not possess.
(sp)/l.c.--(A.) De Tocqueville, Democracy in America (ital)

Corrected Version:

A MARKED-UP MANUSCRIPT

An American, instead of going in a leisure hour to
dance merrily at some place of public resort, as
the fellows of his calling continue to do throughout the greater part of Europe, shuts himself up at
home to drink. He thus enjoys two pleasures; he
can go on thinking of his business, and he can get
decently drunk by his own fireside. . .

In America I saw the freest and most enlightened
men, placed in the happiest circumstances which
the world affords. [Yet] it seemed to me as if a
cloud habitually hung upon their brow, and I
thought them serious and most sad even in their
pleasures . . . , forever brooding over advantages
they do not possess.
--Alexis de Tocqueville, Democracy in America

4 First-Level Editing: Content

> No one can write decently who is
> distrustful of the reader's intelligence or
> whose attitude is patronizing.
> —E. B. White

Writing is only half of communicating; someone must also read and understand what you have written. Let's explore some ways to make your writing readable and understandable.

Write to Your Audience

Your audience may consist of many individuals, none of whom you know. Or you may be writing to a specific individual whom you know well. In either case, what you know about your readers' tastes, interests, and levels of sophistication should determine your approach to a subject and the tone of your writing.

Approach

Have you told readers what they need to know? When you're immersed in a subject, it's easy to lose sight of how much background the reader needs to grasp your ideas. Identify the readers you're addressing and aim for common ground. Start from a place that's familiar to everyone, then gradually introduce new information. In general, it's important to bring readers along one step at a time. If you give them too much information, too abruptly, they may abandon the effort.

When writing for a lay audience, define unfamiliar terms or concepts. Avoid such stiff and long-winded definitions as the following:

> Caisson disease is a disorder in divers and tunnel workers caused by returning too rapidly from high pressure to atmospheric pressure, characterized by pains in the joints, cramps, paralysis, and eventual death unless treated by gradual decompression.

Instead, you might define by the context:

> Divers who work underwater experience severe cramps and pains in their joints if they return to the surface too rapidly. This condition, known as caisson disease or "the bends," is prevented by increasing the time allowed for decompression.

or parenthetically:

> The divers return to the surface gradually in order to avoid "the bends" (severe cramping and pains in their joints).

Analogies and examples, especially ones with human interest, help make the subject matter accessible to a lay audience. Whatever your topic, explain the unknown in terms of the known.

> When a man sits with a pretty girl for an hour, it seems like a minute. But let him sit on a hot stove for a minute, and it's longer than an hour. That's relativity.—*Albert Einstein*

When writing for an audience of experts, your "launch point" is different. Only newly coined terms or those from another discipline require explanation. Expert audiences want the facts: what something costs, the size of the market, whether you can scale up from prototype to mass production. For a knowledgeable audience, you can economize on background information, but don't skimp on essential details.

If you know your audience is sympathetic, you don't have to sell your ideas. But an unconvinced or antagonistic audience requires different handling. Present your strongest arguments with no waffling. Imagine yourself as the reader; what counter-arguments or questions would you raise? Answer them. Does your answer raise other questions? Answer those, too.

Do you make recommendations? If so, present them early. Readers may become impatient following your thought processes step by step, not knowing your conclusions until the end. They want your recommendations up front ("what"), and then how you arrived at them ("why").

Slanted writing erodes your credibility. Avoid making empty claims (*fantastic results*), applying unfriendly labels (*big business, bureaucrat*), or using derogatory words (*fad, spurious*). Back up assertions, or readers will respond with "So what?" or "Why?"

Tone

When you're being interviewed for a job, you use one tone of voice. When you're having lunch with a friend, you use another. Similarly, tone in writing is formal or informal, high pressure or low key, partisan or objective.

A formal, businesslike tone is appropriate when reporting to a superior or applying for a job. The same tone would seem distant and cold when communicating with colleagues or seeking employees' suggestions. If you want to establish a friendly, informal relationship with readers, use plenty of first and second person (*I, you*). Make the tone conversational by using contractions (*you're, I've*). Don't be afraid to let your humanity show.

If your writing is more formal than you like, take a look at your vocabulary. Expressions like "It did not escape our attention..." instead of "We noticed..." sound pompous. Make your writing less stuffy with the following changes.

STUFFY:		BETTER:
accomplish	....	do
advise	....	tell
am in possession of	....	have
anticipate	....	expect
application	....	use (noun)
ascertain	....	find
by the name of	....	named
caused injuries to	....	injured
concerning	....	about
construct, fabricate	....	build
deem	....	think
desire	....	want
disclose	....	show
endeavor	....	try
ensuing	....	following
eschew	....	avoid
forward (verb)	....	send, mail
furnish	....	give
have need for	....	need
in lieu of	....	instead of
in the event that	....	if
indicate	....	show
initiate, commence	....	begin
is of the opinion	....	believes, thinks
kindly	....	please
lengthy	....	long
locate	....	find
methodology	....	methods
not too distant future	....	soon
partially	....	partly

STUFFY:	BETTER:
presently	now
prior to	before
procure	get
pursuant to	following, after, since
request	ask

A tone that is firm, honest, and reasoned fits most situations. Condescension ("As you should have been able to figure out by now...") and breezy intimacy ("We all know why that happened...") have no place in most writing. Irony and sarcasm backfire in the hands of all but the most skilled writers. Above all, be consistent by maintaining the desired tone.

> You can write about anything, and if you write well enough, even the reader with no intrinsic interest in the subject will become involved.—*Tracy Kidder*

Bias-free Writing. When the first edition of *Rewrite Right!* was published, bias-free writing was being hotly debated. Gradually the "person" jokes went stale and disappeared. Today most writers agree that it's just plain smart to remove bias from writing. The goal is to communicate, and that's hard to do if your words offend readers. The following guidelines will help remove bias from your writing.

• Do not mention race, gender, age, or disability unless it is pertinent. For example, look for the hidden assumptions behind marveling about an older person who runs or plays

tennis. Is a sedentary life the norm for everyone over 60?
I hope not!

- Avoid stereotypes and labels.

    Biased: The company picnic will be open to all employees,
    their wives, and families.
    Neutral: The company picnic will be open to all employees,
    their spouses, friends, and families.

- Use parallel treatment.

    Mr. Waxman and Ms. Stone, *not* Mr. Waxman and Linda

- Find substitutes for words that may be insensitive or confusing, such as the word *man* or masculine pronouns.

BIASED:	NEUTRAL:
anchorman	anchor
businessman	executive, manager, entrepreneur, merchant
chairman	chair
congressman	member of Congress
councilman	council member
draftsman	drafter
foreman	supervisor
layman	layperson, lay audience
layman's terms	non-technical language
mailman	letter carrier, postal clerk
man (noun)	human, humanity, human beings, persons, civilization, human race

BIASED:	NEUTRAL:
man (verb)	staff (e.g., *staff the booth*), operate, run, work
man-hours	hours, work-hours, staff-hours
manpower	personnel, staff, workers
repairman	service rep
salesman	salesperson, marketing rep
spokesman	representative, spokesperson
statesman	diplomat
workmen	workers

When you're referring to a specific male member of Congress or committee chair, it's acceptable to identify the individual as Congressman Ortega or Chairman Tyler. But if the term covers both women and men, or if it is open-ended, use a neutral term.

> The committee will elect a new chair.
> *not* The committee will elect a new chairman.

Here are ways to avoid using masculine pronouns.

> **Biased:** Each applicant must submit his resume.
> **Neutral:** Each applicant must submit a resume.

> **Biased:** The consumer can stretch disposable income if he refrains from impulse buying.
> **Neutral:** Consumers can stretch disposable income by refraining from impulse buying.

> **Awkward:** Has someone lost his or her gloves?
> **Better:** Has someone lost a pair of gloves?

Make your writing sensitive to both subject and reader. This doesn't mean removing all wit, flavor, and variety. You can remove offensive words and biased assumptions without resorting to clumsy solutions. As you become more aware of the subtle ways that bias creeps into writing, you will find easy and natural ways to make language bias-free.

Have a Plan

Put your ideas into writing before trying to organize them. If you're worrying about where they fit, you may lose some thoughts. Jot down the subjects in any order, regardless of importance: main points, minor points, examples, comparisons, background material. Write down whatever comes to mind about the topic. (See Outlining, p. 6.)

> Write freely and as rapidly as possible and throw the whole thing on paper. Never correct or rewrite until the whole thing is down.—*John Steinbeck*

When the "dump" of ideas from your head to the page or computer screen is complete, organize those thoughts into a logical scheme. In effect, you're creating a map that says to readers, "We're now at A; we're heading for B. Here's our route." Without such a plan, information is a jumbled heap of facts. By establishing a skeleton on which to hang details, you make the information accessible and more easily remembered.

Organizing

Organizing ideas is a two-step task: (1) group similar subjects, and (2) link the groups logically.

Grouping and Labeling. Readers find it difficult to grasp too many packets of information at one time. By combining similar items or ideas under a unifying concept, you give them a handle on the information.

Suppose you were asked to evaluate several office copiers. You could group your findings under labels that identify pertinent aspects:

- Major Features (speed, appearance, size)

- Additional Capabilities (document feeder, reduction, collation, stapling)

- Cost (initial, long-term, lease vs. buy)

- Maintenance (average time between service calls)

- Warranties (guarantee period, coverage)

Within these categories, you could label specific features as "Advantages" or "Disadvantages." You could also identify which capabilities are important for your office. Your approach depends on your purpose, but grouping and labeling make the information easier to absorb.

> The first rule of style is to have something to say. The second rule of style is to control yourself when, by chance, you have two things to say; say first one, then the other, not both at the same time.—*George Polya*

Linking the Groups. Next, link the groups of ideas in a logical scheme. The framework that best suits your purpose will take into account your readers' needs and interests and how ideas naturally come together. Here are five approaches to imposing order on writing.

STEPS IN A PROCESS: Describe procedures, step by step, like a recipe. *Use in instructions, operator's manuals, how-to articles.*

CHRONOLOGICAL: Trace the sequence of events: what happened and when. *Use in progress reports, biographical or historical sketches, accident reports, legal depositions, trip reports.*

ANALYTICAL: Present data, draw conclusions. *Use in annual reports, feasibility studies, investment memos, market surveys, consumer reports.*

COMPARISON: Emphasize similarities and differences or advantages and disadvantages. *Use in feasibility studies, surveys of competition, product comparisons, building site evaluations.*

GEOGRAPHICAL: Describe subjects by region. *Use in market surveys, sales reports, travel articles.*

Within such loose frameworks, you have still more choices about how to organize your information. For example:

- Most to least important (or vice versa)

- Least to most controversial

- Negative to positive (or vice versa)

- Deductive reasoning (from general to specific) or inductive reasoning (from particular to general)

When you are making a recommendation, it often pays to begin with your most important point. However, "least to most controversial" may be necessary if your readers need to be persuaded. "Negative to positive" will avoid your being charged with dodging issues; it also leaves readers on a positive note.

Typically, several methods of organization are used within one document, possibly within a single paragraph. An annual report, for example, could announce record earnings (*most to least important*), introduce new products (*analytical*), describe regional operations (*geographical*), report on the competition (*comparison*), and recommend how shareholders vote (*least to most controversial*).

Make each paragraph a coherent unit with a limited and well-defined purpose. One thought: one paragraph. Use the first sentence (the topic sentence) to tell what the paragraph is about (the thesis); relate subsequent sentences to the thesis. For example:

> Men make history and not the other way round. [Topic Sentence] In periods where there is no leadership, society

stands still. Progress occurs when courageous, skillful lead-
ers seize the opportunity to change things for the better.
—*Harry S. Truman*

As you edit for logical organization, you may find an idea out
of place or a major point buried in the middle of a paragraph.
Rearrange the sentences until the pieces fit together smoothly.

Format

Format is important in identifying main topics and supporting
ideas or information. Use spacing, numerals, headings, and
underlining, italics, or boldface to emphasize key ideas. By effi-
ciently identifying the main points, you give busy readers the
basic thrust of your presentation.

Grab Their Attention

The attention of your audience may be assured if you are writing about a topic of interest to them—or if it's required reading. But even with a captive audience, clear, vigorous writing is a courtesy well worth observing.

Titles

The title is your first chance to catch the reader's attention. Is it informative? There should be no question what the subject is, yet the title needn't be dull or wordy. "An Overview of the Structural and Conceptual Characteristics of Future Planning Systems" strikes out on both counts. "Planning: System or Chaos?" might get you to first base.

A short title is easier to remember, so boil it down to as few words as possible, and then play with them a little. Does it help to phrase the title as a question? Perhaps the main title can be the attention grabber and the subtitle can flesh out the subject. Sometimes a play on words is effective, but being too cute is a hazard. Notice titles that you come across in your reading. What makes them work?

Headings

Headings are your next chance to catch the reader's eye. They provide information as well as visual breaks; they reveal the structure of your text, making it easier to locate information or follow the flow of ideas. A busy reader can skim headings to find the sections of most interest.

Headings can be single words:

Introduction	Conclusions
Analysis	Summary

phrases:

> Tracking Regional Performance
> Absenteeism under the Flexitime Program

complete sentences:

> Regional performance is uneven.
> Flexitime reduces absenteeism.

or questions:

> Are regional sales uniform?
> Will Flexitime improve productivity?

Make the style of comparable headings parallel. Use similar verb forms, noun phrases, or complete sentences to help a reader understand the relationship between different sections. Compare the following groups of headings. The first is a hodgepodge of verbs, nouns, and sentences; it's hard to see any relation between them. The second has parallel forms of action verbs that clearly present the topic (ways to use a video recorder).

AWKWARD:	PARALLEL:
Training Technicians	Train Technicians
Use Your Recorder to Screen New Employees	Screen New Employees
Time-and-Motion Studies	Document Time-and-Motion Studies
How to Improve Quality Control	Improve Quality Control

(See p. 132 for more about parallelism.)

Headings can be centered, flush left, indented, italicized, or boldface; they can be all capital letters or uppercase and lowercase. The text that follows a heading either starts a new line or is run in on the same line as the heading. Make the format of your headings consistent. The following examples are themselves illustrations of two different formats.

Here is one example of a heading format:

FIRST ORDER HEADINGS (all caps, centered)

Second Order Headings (italics)
Text follows on next line.
Third Order Headings (boldface): Text run in on same line.

Here is another heading format example:

FIRST ORDER HEADINGS (all caps, flush left)

Second Order Headings (boldface): Text run in on same line.
    Third Order Headings (italics): Indented, text run in on same line.

Openings

Writers often meander before getting down to business. If you're one of them, you may find that what you've written in the second or third paragraph is your strongest opening.

The goal is to get to the point quickly. Readers want to know what you are writing about and why it matters. This doesn't mean beginning with a plodding "The purpose of this memo (report, article) is to…." An effective beginning incorporates purpose indirectly, perhaps even dramatically.

> Isolation is one of the biggest challenges facing employees who work at home. Networking may give them instant communication with colleagues in Singapore and Riyadh, yet fail to provide the energy of direct human interaction.

Readers know what to expect from such an opening. It states the problem and suggests the scope of what follows.

Jumping right in with a recommendation is another approach.

> A mandatory day in the office every week offsets the isolation of working alone at home. Employees enjoy flexible hours and an easy commute, while management retains more direct control.

Emphasis

Are details supplied in proportion to importance? Is your main thesis diluted by lesser points? When you know more about a minor point than a major one, you may be tempted to display your knowledge with lots of words. Resist the temptation.

The way you construct sentences also subordinates one idea to another. Notice the change in emphasis in the following sentences.

> The new assembly line has produced some lemons, but genuine progress has been made.

> Genuine progress has been made, although the new assembly line has produced some lemons.

You can emphasize important points in other ways, too.

- BULLETS: Make short items stand out

- UNDERLINING OR ITALICS: Focus on topic sentences or stress specific words or phrases

- CAPITAL LETTERS: Provide a visual break or identify a brand name

- INDENTATIONS: Set off quotations or bulleted information

- NUMBERING: Identify groupings

An occasional question-and-answer format draws the reader into your line of thought.

> Is Flexitime the only way to reduce absenteeism? Obviously not.

A colon focuses attention on what follows.

> Leasing equipment has one major advantage: flexibility.

The order in which you present items also creates emphasis. Notice how the following sentences have a built-in kicker at the end.

> There are several good protections against temptation, but the surest is cowardice.—*Mark Twain*

> If you would know the value of money, go and try to borrow some.—*Poor Richard*

> Injustice is relatively easy to bear; what stings is justice. —*H. L. Mencken*

Variety

A series of declarative sentences (subject-verb, subject-verb) soon puts readers to sleep.

> Company profits fell 14% during the last quarter. Analysts attributed the decrease to foreign competition. Recovery is anticipated in the coming reporting period.... (snore)

You can break away from such monotony by varying sentence structure, sentence length, and paragraph length.

Vary Sentence Structure. Sentences are classified as simple, compound, and complex. A *simple sentence* is a subject and predicate (in other words, an independent clause—one that can stand by itself).

> <u>The polls</u> <u>closed at 8 p.m.</u>
> subject   predicate

A *compound sentence* is two or more independent clauses.

> The polls closed at 8 p.m., and
> independent clause

> the ballots were counted within an hour.
> independent clause

A *complex sentence* is an independent clause plus one or more dependent clauses (a dependent clause cannot stand by itself as a separate sentence).

> Although the polls closed at 8 p.m.,
> dependent clause

> we had counted the ballots by 9:00.
> independent clause

As you can see, each type of sentence has a different "personality." Simple sentences are a good device for making short or emphatic statements. Compound sentences work well with two closely related elements or ideas. Complex sentences are good for presenting background information or for subordinating one idea to another.

The following examples show how some eminent people have used all three types. Notice the variety of ways these sentences begin; different beginnings also make writing more interesting.

Simple Sentences:

> There's no reason to be the richest man in the cemetery. You can't do any business from there.—*Colonel Sanders*

> Having two bathrooms ruined the capacity to cooperate. —*Margaret Mead*

> Nothing so needs reforming as other people's habits.
> —*Mark Twain*

> A clear conscience is usually the sign of a bad memory.
> —*Anonymous*

Compound Sentences:

> I don't know the key to success, but the key to failure is trying to please everybody.—*Bill Cosby*

> I tape, therefore I am.—*Studs Terkel*

> The cost of living is going up, and the chance of living is going down.—*Flip Wilson*

Complex Sentences:

> Fanaticism consists in redoubling your effort when you have forgotten your aim.—*George Santayana*

> A government is the only known vessel that leaks from the top.—*James Reston*

> Read over your compositions and, when you meet a passage which you think is particularly fine, strike it out.
> —*Samuel Johnson*

Vary Sentence Length. Short sentences are effective for introducing a new subject, long ones for developing a point. Modern writing tends to favor sentences of roughly 20 words. But if a sentence is well crafted and not overloaded with ideas, you can stretch those boundaries with an occasional long sentence. Use word-processing programs that analyze sentence and word length to determine readability.

Vary Paragraph Length. How long are your paragraphs? Generous amounts of white space hold the readers' interest and avoid visual monotony. They also avoid intimidating readers with solid blocks of type.

Busy people often rely on a quick look at the opening of a paragraph to determine if they want to read the rest. It follows that more of the document will be read if it consists of short paragraphs. However, lots of one- or two-sentence paragraphs become monotonous and tend to de-emphasize everything on the page. Reserve the shortest paragraphs (even as short as one sentence) for the points you want to stand out.

Closings

> ...go on till you come to the end; then stop.
> *—Lewis Carroll*

How do you know when you're at the end? If you have clearly understood your objective in writing, you probably also know when you've achieved that purpose. You will have presented the information in digestible chunks, included supporting arguments, or provided explanations and examples. In short, because you knew where you were going, you will know when you've arrived.

What remains is to button it up. Are the conclusions you want readers to draw from your evidence clear? Present one last compelling argument to reinforce the main points. In long documents, summarize important ideas in a different way, rather than repeating yourself. Where appropriate, indicate the next steps to be taken. Make the ending provide a sense of completeness.

Stephen Jay Gould closed an essay on the search for intelligent life in outer space with a question.

> Ultimately, however, I must justify the attempt at such a long shot simply by stating that a positive result would be the most cataclysmic event in our entire intellectual history. Curiosity impels, and makes us human. Might it impel others as well?

In "The Gift of Wilderness," Wallace Stegner hammers home his message in a long and powerful last sentence.

> Instead of easing air-pollution controls in order to postpone the education of the automobile industry; instead of opening our forests to greatly increased timber cutting; instead of running our national parks to please and profit the concessionaires; instead of violating our wilderness areas by allowing oil and mineral exploration with rigs and roads and seismic detonations, we might bear in mind what those precious places are: playgrounds, schoolrooms, laboratories, yes, but above all shrines, in which we can learn to know both the natural world and ourselves, and be at least half reconciled to what we see.

Make It Clear

Trouble in writing clearly...reflects troubled thinking, usually an incomplete grasp of the facts or their meaning.—*Barbara Tuchman*

Clear thinking is a prerequisite for clear writing. But even if your thoughts are muddled when you start, the act of writing often clarifies thinking. Your real purpose may become obvious only after you have struggled to write about it.

Writing is clear when readers get the point quickly and can follow supporting arguments. Any ambiguity or vagueness that gets in the way is bad writing.

Avoid Ambiguity

Have you left a reader in doubt as to the meaning of critical words?

Ambiguous: Child killers can be rehabilitated.

"Child killers" could mean people who kill children or killers who are themselves children. Your meaning may be so clear to you that you fail to see the possibility of other interpretations.

Ambiguous: She is helping the prisoners get off drugs and recording books for the blind.

This sentence suggests that the prisoners need to kick their habit of recording books for the blind, as well as their drug habit. Rewrite to avoid such booby traps.

Have you omitted any necessary words? Readers might wonder about the meaning of the following sentences:

Phil loves power more than his wife.

San Diego is farther from Los Angeles than Santa Barbara.

Less confusing versions would be:

Phil loves power more than he loves his wife.
or Phil loves power more than his wife does.

San Diego is farther from Los Angeles than Santa Barbara is.

Have you omitted necessary punctuation? The following sentences should have commas to prevent misreading.

After eating the negotiators returned to the bargaining session.

When the headlights are on an indicator light in the push button illuminates the switch.

As children grow the specific emotional lessons they are ready for include...

Even though I was young when she told me that I understood her meaning completely.

An omitted hyphen in a heading can also be misleading. There's a big difference between "Attack Dog Training" and "Attack-Dog Training." (See pp. 102 for more discussion of hyphens.)

Does the position of a word or phrase create ambiguity? In the following example, the employees might be in for an unpleasant situation.

Ambiguous: I have discussed how to fill the empty containers with my employees.

Clear: I have discussed with my employees how to fill the empty containers.

Revise Unclear References

Are your references confusing? When you write *it* or *they* or *her*, do readers know what those pronouns refer to? In other words, are the antecedents of the pronouns clear?

Ambiguous: John Doe is the son of a plumbing supply salesman who died when he was 10.

Who was 10, the salesman or his son? We can make a good guess, but we shouldn't have to. Logic tells us that we must leapfrog back to the word *son* to find the correct antecedent for the pronoun *he*. Avoid putting readers through such gyrations (and giving them a belly laugh at your expense) by making sure each pronoun refers clearly and correctly to its antecedent.

The best solution may be to avoid using a pronoun.

Clear: John Doe, the son of a plumbing supply salesman who died when John was 10...

Here are some other examples of unclear references and ways to correct them.

This, that, these, those. Are these words followed by a noun? If not, they are probably faulty references.

Unclear: The staff has begun analyzing the chain of events that produced the increase in sales. This was long overdue.

This could refer to the analysis or to the increase in sales.

Clear: The staff has begun analyzing the chain of events that produced the increase in sales. This long overdue analysis will shape our marketing strategy.

Who. Does *who* refer to the preceding noun? In the following example, the preceding noun is *board*.

Unclear: The chairman of the board, who will be available for comment...

Will the board or the chairman be available?

Clear: The board chairman, who will be available...

It. Is the word that *it* refers to actually in the sentence?

Unclear: On the second day, the patient's knee was better, and on the third day, it had completely disappeared.

The word *it* obviously refers to a physical problem that isn't stated.

Clear: On the second day, the patient's knee was better, and on the third day, the pain had disappeared completely.

Which. Does an intervening phrase make the reader uncertain of the meaning?

Unclear: The report of the commission, which attracted so much media attention...

Does *which* refer to the commission or the report?

Clear: The commission's report, which attracted...

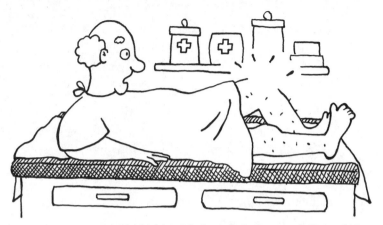

...on the third day, it had completely disappeared. (See p. 56.)

Frequently, removing prepositional phrases such as "of the commission" removes uncertainty.

Be Specific

Vague words fail to convey information. A general statement like "Product X saves you money" is unconvincing. It leaves unanswered the question "How?" Readers want the specifics: miles per gallon, infrequency of repair, warranties. Writing "She is a good employee" suggests general satisfaction with performance but provides no way to confirm that opinion. The more vivid and precise your words, the better the readers will understand and remember them.

> **Specific:** She learns quickly and is eager to increase her skills. When we acquired a Zaplex, she was the first to master the system. Her help in training the rest of the staff proved invaluable.

Being precise does not require that you be long-winded. One exact word often replaces several inexact ones. Furthermore, you can be precise with the plain words that many people use every day.

Vague:	Specific:
a better position	a 23% increase in profits
sanitary conditions	safe drinking water
extenuating circumstances	a broken leg
the present writer	I
a plumbing malfunction	a leaky faucet

Examples are a good way to make your writing specific. If you're reporting on the pros and cons of Flexitime, don't stop at citing "improved employee morale" as one of the benefits.

> Employees say they like having time off during the day. They use it for everything from teacher conferences to Christmas shopping. Medical appointments, physical-fitness programs, and special events such as a concert or ball game are easier to fit into their lives. Many add that they appreciate just being able to break up the daily routine.

Abstract words can highlight underlying concepts (e.g., productivity, labor relations). But unless you tie down the abstractions with particulars (number of units produced, freedom from strikes), readers have to guess at your meaning.

Syndicated columnist Donella Meadows illustrates the importance of vivid language. As she explores the idea that dry writing may be the reason why environmentalists have failed to convey the urgency of the global situation, she presents three versions of the same viewpoint.

> **First Version:** "Our massive tampering with the world's inter-dependent web of life—coupled with the environmental damage inflicted by deforestation, species loss, and climate change—could trigger widespread adverse effects, including unpredictable collapses of critical biological systems and interactions and dynamics we only imperfectly understand. Uncertainty over the extent of these effects cannot excuse complacency or delay in facing the threats."

Second Version: "People are devastating the environment. We are destroying forests, driving species to extinction, and changing the climate. Whole plant and animal systems may die before we understand how they function. Since we don't understand what we are doing, it is inexcusable for us to dismiss or ignore signs of danger."

Third Version: "We are wrecking nature without understanding how it works or how it supports us."

Meadows has a point.

Use Transitional Words

Certain words tell the reader what to expect. *But* or *however* warns that you're changing direction; *therefore* spotlights a conclusion. Without such transitions, the bridge between sentences is missing, and readers have no time to grasp the full meaning of one idea before the next one hits them.

Confusing: Not all patients do well; some fail completely. The overall results are good.

Clear: Not all patients do well; some fail completely. However, the overall results are good.

Jacques Barzun describes transitional words as the guiding touch to the elbow of someone you are piloting through new sights. Use the "guiding touch" of transitional words to pilot your readers.

TRANSITIONAL WORDS

To indicate a conclusion:	*thus, accordingly, therefore, so, hence, as a result, consequently*
To introduce examples:	*for instance, namely, for example, to illustrate*
To build a case:	*also, similarly, in addition, as well as, furthermore, moreover*
To change direction or show contrast:	*on the other hand, however, on the contrary, even though, nonetheless, conversely, but, yet*
To indicate time, place, or order:	*finally, first, next, then, further, meanwhile, above all, still, again*

Be Positive About Negatives
Multiple negatives create confusion.

Snyder did not believe the lack of funding was unimportant.

Just what *did* Snyder believe? Make your reader's job easier by recasting the negatives in a positive form.

Snyder believed the lack of funding was important.

If your sentence loses some of its punch when restated positively, find ways to reinject emphasis or drama.

Snyder believed the lack of funding could be critical.

Double negatives can be ungrammatical (Don't do nothing illegal) or grammatical (The plan is not without merit). But even grammatical ones may be confusing.

```
not unaware = aware
```

Use double negatives sparingly and only when a positive statement fails to convey your meaning.

Misplaced negatives are also troublesome. Note the shift of meaning with the change in placement of "not" in the following example.

Misplaced: It is <u>not</u> expected that tomorrow's speech will deal with the economy but will be confined to...

Correct: It is expected that tomorrow's speech will <u>not</u> deal with the economy but will be confined to...

Review the use of negatives as you edit by looking for "not" and "un-." Is a sentence improved by changing negative to positive?

Using antonyms is a concise way to make negative statements positive.

He did not pay attention to the request.
He ignored the request.

The office will not be open on Labor Day.
The office will be closed on Labor Day.

They were not present during the interrogation.
They were absent during the interrogation.

Benzene is not safe to ingest.
Benzene is highly toxic.

Most words beginning with *in-* are negative: ineligible, inappropriate, inaudible. But some actually have positive meanings and should be used carefully: invaluable, inflammable, indebted, inhabitable.

And of course, double negatives can sometimes be fun.

I live in terror of not being misunderstood.—*Oscar Wilde*

5 First-Level Editing: Style

> A good style should show no sign of effort.
> What is written should seem like a happy
> accident.—*W. Somerset Maugham*

"Happy accidents" follow when you remove surplus words, avoid jargon and clichés, use words correctly, and choose vivid language.

Trim the Lard

Pruning extra words is one of the biggest jobs in editing. As you read each sentence, ask yourself which words could be dropped. Many of the guidelines presented in this book help tighten writing; the following suggestions for removing redundancies and padding will contribute to the goal.

Redundancies

Is your writing cluttered with words that have the same meaning (basic fundamentals, separate and distinct, near the vicinity of, exact same, reiterate again, various different, and general consensus of opinion)? Not all redundancies are so blatant. "In addition to...also" and "estimated at about... " are common ways of covering the same ground twice. Here are some others.

Redundant: The <u>age</u> of this tree is more than 1000 years <u>old</u>.
Trimmed: This tree is more than 1000 years old.

Redundant: His remarks were <u>limited only</u> to...
Trimmed: His remarks were limited to...

Redundant: An <u>additional</u> title was <u>added</u> to the list.
Trimmed: Another title was added to the list.

Redundant: The <u>reason</u> I'm late is <u>because</u> my car wouldn't start.
Trimmed: I'm late because my car wouldn't start.

Some expressions are not only repetitious but nonsensical. An "unsubstantiated rumor" suggests there could be a substantiated rumor. Writing "your own autobiography"—could you write anyone else's? Trim such excess words from your writing.

REDUNDANT EXPRESSIONS
(Delete the italicized words)

Adjectives
absolute necessity
active consideration
advance reservations
both alike
close proximity
complete monopoly
conclusive proof
end result
final outcome
free gift
general rule
new recruit
past history
personal opinion
positive identification
proposed plan
root cause
single unit
temporary reprieve
usual custom

Nouns
Capitol *building*
component *parts*
doctorate *degree*
weather *conditions*

Prepositional Phrases
brief *in duration*
classified *into groups*
estimated at *about*
few *in number*
filled *to capacity*
green *in color*
large *in size*

plan *in advance*
rectangular *in shape*
1 a.m. *in the morning*

Adverbs
completely surround
eliminate *entirely*
might *possibly*
mutually agreeable
really dangerous

Prefixes, Suffixes
*ir*regardless
to the west*ward*
*un*relentlessly

Verb Tails
assemble *together*
cancel *out*
connect *up*
continue *on*
enclosed *herein*
face *up to*
follow *after*
hurry *up*
join *together*
made *out* of
merge *together*
visit *with*

Repetitive Phrases
(Choose one part)
any and all
exact same
if and when
new all-time record high
unless and until

Padding

Make each word carry its own weight. "There is room in the basic unit for up to two disk drives" conveys no more than "The basic unit can hold two disk drives." "As of now we have no progress to report" starts with three clutter words.

Tightening windy expressions saves on printing, reduces reading time, and improves the likelihood that the document will actually be read. Here are some ways to streamline language.

PADDED:	TRIMMED:
a large (small) number of	many, few
ahead of schedule	early
along the lines of	like
at a later date	later
draw to your attention	show, point out
during the course of	during, while
had occasion to be	was
have need for	need
in advance of	before
in connection with	about
in regard (relation) to	about
make use of	use
not in a position to	unable to, cannot
on a regular basis	regularly
on two separate occasions	twice
put in an appearance	appeared
retain a position as	remain
such time as	when
take into consideration	consider
the majority of	most
until such time as	until

The following types of sentences are cluttered with too many words.

The...of

> The manufacture of paint is...
> Paint manufacture is...
>
> The level of crime
> The crime level

There are...who/that

> There are some circumstances that require...
> Some circumstances require...

It was/It is

> It was the Personnel Manager who issued the pink slips.
> The Personnel Manager issued the pink slips.
>
> It is necessary to sign...
> You need to (or must) sign...

Removing surplus words forces you to think about exactly what you want to say. Expressing your ideas more accurately may make total word count go up instead of down. That's all right. The goal is not simply to lop off words but to make all of them work for you.

> I believe more in the scissors
> than I do in the pencil.—*Truman Capote*

Know Your Words

The almost-right word is not good enough. "Deprecate" won't do if you mean "depreciate" or "prerequisite" if you mean "perquisite." A spell-checker won't keep you from using the wrong word, so make a habit of looking up meanings in a good dictionary. Read respected authors to develop a feeling for the correct use of words.

Ordinary words used precisely are more impressive than big words used sloppily. But even ordinary words can be used imprecisely. Do you write "always" when you should write "usually," "never" when "seldom" is more accurate, or "exactly" when "nearly" is a better word?

If you can't decide which of several words to use, try my method—put the alternatives in brackets. Later, when you return to the bracketed spot, the choice may be easier.

Commonly Misused Words

Affect/effect. *Affect* is primarily a verb, meaning to have an influence upon (How did the pills affect you?). *Effect* as a noun means result or consequence (The effect of the pills was easy to see); as a verb, it means to bring about (The pills effected a cure).

Aggravate. To make worse; not a substitute for *irritate* or *annoy*.

Anxious. Uneasy, apprehensive. Appropriate where apprehension or concern is implied; *eager* is the word to use when something is earnestly desired.

Claim. Many careful writers prefer the verbs *assert* or *maintain*.

Complement/compliment. These words have both noun and verb forms. *Complement* means to go well with or satisfy a need. *Compliment* means to praise.

Comprise. To include or be composed of. Avoid *is comprised of*; instead, use *comprises* or *consists of*.

> The whole comprises the parts.
> The parts constitute the whole.

Convince/persuade. *Convince* involves a state of mind (convince that), *persuade* a course of action (persuade to).

> She convinced me that the Earth is flat.
> He persuaded me to join the Flat Earth Society.

Dilemma. Use *dilemma* to indicate two choices, each undesirable. To describe a generally difficult situation, use *predicament*.

Equally. Use only where equality pertains.

> **Wrong:** The night shift performs equally as well as the day shift. (To correct the sentence, delete equally.)

> **Right:** The sum was divided equally among the heirs.

Farther/further. Use *farther* with physical distance. (He can see farther than I can.) To indicate extent or degree, use *further*. (Let's study the matter further.)

Fewer/less. Use *fewer* with things that can be counted (individual numbers or units); use *less* with quantity.

> Fewer mistakes, less embarrassment.

Fulsome. Means disgusting, excessive, insincere. Don't reach for this word when you mean plentiful.

Irregardless. Use *regardless* or *irrespective*, not this mixture of the two.

It's. Means *it is* or *it has*. The correct possessive pronoun is *its*. (See p. 92.)

Like/as. Use *like* with nouns or pronouns (She is tall, like her father). Use *as* with phrases (Profits rose, as in the previous quarter).

Literally. Means really or actually; don't use as an intensifier. Delete from a sentence like "He literally exploded when he heard the news."

Percentage. Avoid using as a substitute for *some*.

Preventive. Not *preventative*.

Principal. (1) An adjective meaning chief or main; (2) a noun designating a school official; (3) in a legal context, an important person. Often confused with *principle*, which is a rule or fundamental truth.

Respectively. Singly, in the order stated. The correct word in the complimentary close of a letter is *respectfully*.

-self. Correct if adding emphasis (I saw the Pope himself) or as a reflexive pronoun (She hurt herself). Not interchangeable with a pronoun.

> **Wrong:** Riley and myself are heading the team.

> **Right:** Riley and I are heading the team.

Suspicion. A noun, not a verb. You have a suspicion, or you suspect something, but you don't suspicion something.

That/which. Use *that* to introduce a restrictive clause and *which* to introduce a nonrestrictive or parenthetical one.

> Your manuscript is both good and original; but the part that is good is not original, and the part that is original is not good.—*Samuel Johnson*

> My decision, which didn't come easily, is final.

Unique. An overworked word, often misused for *rare* or *notable*.

Incorrect plurals are a common source of error. Words with Latin roots (*data, criteria, phenomena, media*) have irregular singular and plural forms: *phenomenon* (singular) and *phenomena* (plural). Since these words are not made plural by adding *s* or *es*, many people don't know whether they are using a singular or plural word. They make two kinds of mistakes:

• Using the plural form of the word when singular is called for

  Age was the sole criteria for determining eligibility. (Make that **criterion**.)

• Using a singular verb with a plural form of the word

  The media was excluded from the meeting. (Make that **were**.)

Add professional polish to your writing by using singular and plural words correctly. Refer to the "Irregular Plurals" list for help.

IRREGULAR PLURALS

Singular:	Plural:
alumna (fem.)	alumnae
alumnus (masc.)	alumni (masc. or both sexes)
analysis	analyses
antenna	antennas (radio, TV), antennae (insects)
apparatus	apparatus *or* apparatuses
appendix	appendixes *or* appendices
bacterium	bacteria
crisis	crises
criterion	criteria
curriculum	curricula *or* curriculums
genus	genera
index	indexes (publishing), indices (math)
kibbutz	kibbutzim
matrix	matrices *or* matrixes
medium	media
millennium	millennia
phenomenon	phenomena
radius	radii
stratum	strata
symposium	symposia *or* symposiums
synopsis	synopses
vertebra	vertebrae *or* vertebras

matrix + matrix = matrices

Cut Clichés and Hackneyed Expressions

Words that are overworked lose their force. When every event is a "crisis," it's hard to get worked up about another one.

Voguish words are a poor vehicle for fresh ideas; be wary of expressions that seem to appear, unbeckoned.

> Modern writing at its worst...consists in gumming together long strips of words which have already been set in order by someone else and making the results presentable by sheer humbug.
> —George Orwell

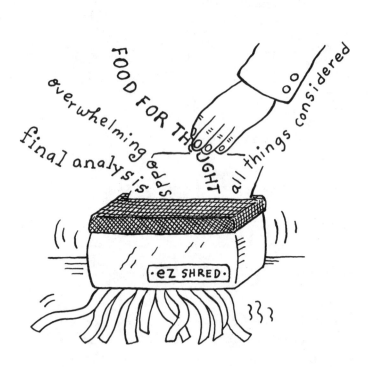

If an expression is both hackneyed and garbled, you are vulnerable to smirks or outright guffaws.

> Keep a stiff upper hand.
> Opening up a whole can of wax...
> Chafing at the bit...
> It created a human cry.
> They just shrugged their noses.
> He's a ragged individualist.

By avoiding clichés altogether, you appear more professional. Shun the expressions on the "Overworked Expressions" list.

OVERWORKED EXPRESSIONS

abreast of the times	drastic action
add insult to injury	due consideration
all things considered	eminently successful
along these lines	equal to the occasion
ample opportunity	exception that proves the rule
as a matter of fact	exercise in futility
at a loss for words	existing conditions
at long last	festive occasion
back burner	few well-chosen words
benefit of the doubt	final analysis
better late than never	finishing touches
bitter end	food for thought
bone of contention	force of circumstance
by the same token	foregone conclusion
capacity crowd	give the green light to
checkered career	grave concern
city fathers	heated argument
considered opinion	herculean efforts
controlling factor	inflationary spiral
crying need	

continued on p. 76

OVERWORKED EXPRESSIONS

in no uncertain terms
in short supply
in this day and age
irreparable loss
it goes without saying
just desserts
keep options open
leave no stone unturned
leave well enough alone
lend a helping hand
long-felt need
marked contrast
moment of truth
more than meets the eye
narrow escape
needs no introduction
one and the same
on more than one occasion
open secret
other things being equal
overwhelming odds

own worst enemy
paramount importance
part and parcel
path of least resistance
regrettable incident
reliable source
remedy the situation
ripe old age
round of applause
second to none
select few
sweeping changes
too numerous to mention
unprecedented situation
untimely end
viable alternative
view with alarm
wave of the future
whole new ball game
you don't have to be a
    rocket scientist

Speak Out

Strive for assertive writing. It is direct and crisp, unburdened by the passive voice, lifeless verbs, and too many qualifiers.

> English is a remarkably clear, flexible, and useful language. We should use it in all of our communications.—*Daniel O'Neal, Jr.*
>
> Hear, hear!—*Jan Venolia*

Use the Active Voice

The passive voice combines a form of the verb *to be* with the past participle of another verb (was submitted, are seen, is urged, were reported, has been completed). When you write in the passive voice, the subject is acted upon.

Passive: The report was written by Molly McCoy.

In the active voice, subject of the sentence is the "doer."

Active: Molly McCoy wrote the report.

Each voice has legitimate uses. The passive voice is appropriate in the following circumstances:

• In technical writing

   The air is heated by being circulated over the coils.

• If the object of the action is more important than the subject

   The meeting was postponed.
   The veteran was awarded the Medal of Honor.

• If the subject is unknown

   The article was unsigned.
   Information was leaked to the press.
   Documents were stolen from the secured area.

• When you want to avoid naming a specific person

   The missing papers were returned.
   The time it takes to write a report is wasted if the report is
      not read.

But in general, the active voice should predominate. Notice how changing from passive to active voice makes the following sentence shorter and livelier.

> **Passive:** It is recommended that special attention be paid to how productivity can be improved by introducing profit-sharing.

Who recommends, pays attention, and improves? We have to guess.

> **Active:** Management should consider how profit-sharing can improve productivity.

Don't shift from active to passive voice mid-sentence.

> **Poor:** Such a program costs little, and many are benefited by it.

> **Better:** Such a program costs little and benefits many.

Avoid Lifeless Verbs

The *Associated Press Guide to Good Writing* points out the pomposity of the word *address* when used for something other than a letter: "Don't address a problem. Instead, deal with it, take it up, consider it, tackle it, cope with it." Good advice!

A lifeless verb brings a sentence to a standstill. *Exist, occur,* and forms of *to be* and *to have* are the worst offenders.

> **Poor:** The Neighborhood Watch program exists in certain communities where there is concern about the crime rate.

> **Better:** The Neighborhood Watch program reflects community concern about the crime rate.

It may seem strange to criticize a verb as essential as *to be*. But sentences built on *to be* are frequently heavy with accompanying baggage.

> The purpose of the report is to provide a means of comparing sales in the four regions.
> The report compares sales in the four regions.

> Cutting government spending is another way to reduce the deficit.
> Cutting government spending also reduces the deficit.

> X is different from Y.
> X differs from Y.

Lifeless verbs are often noun-heavy. When *indicates* becomes *is an indication of*, and *knows* becomes *has a knowledge of*, the pace slows down. Look for word endings like *-ment*, *-tion*, *-ity*, *-ance*, and *-ness*, and give them a shot of adrenaline.

LIFELESS:	LIVELY:
a preference for	prefer
present suggestions for avoiding	suggest ways to avoid
There is a belief among the reporters	The reporters believe
Their response was an indication of	Their response indicated
has a tendency to	tends to

Don't Overqualify
Too many qualifiers weaken writing. E. B. White dramatically described such words as *rather*, *very*, *little*, and *pretty* as "leeches

that infest the pond of prose, sucking the blood of words." No hedging there!

Omit qualifiers that diminish your ideas or are inherently contradictory:

> rather important
> more perfect
> somewhat irresponsible
> almost unique
> very fatal
> moderately exhaustive

Replace qualifiers that just intensify meaning with more descriptive words:

> very important = critical, crucial, central
> really angry = outraged, furious

or just delete them:

> very obstinate = obstinate
> utterly reject = reject
> very ecstatic = ecstatic

Jettison Jargon

Jargon that is the specialized language of a particular science or trade has its proper place. It's an efficient shorthand when writing for an audience that speaks the language.

But some writers use pseudo-technical words simply to impress the reader or to create a verbal smokescreen. Here are the symptoms of such gobbledygook:

- Passive voice
- Prepositional phrases
- Piled-up nouns
- Converted parts of speech
- Abstractions and empty terms
- Buzz words

A murky **passive voice** predominates in jargon-heavy writing. We find neither subject nor actor, just the action: conclusions are reached, relations are improved, and problems are anticipated. (See p. 77.)

Prepositional phrases, unending and uninteresting, often provide the framework of a gobbledygook sentence.

> **Poor:** The root of the problem of negotiation, in which there is the interaction of representatives of groups with conflicting points of view, is the taking of adversarial positions from which retreat is difficult.

> **Better:** When individuals who represent groups with conflicting opinions act as adversaries, retreat from their positions is difficult.

Piled-up nouns proliferate in writing that is full of jargon.

> systems modification effort
> employee productivity improvement possibilities
> highway litter reduction program
> damage situation
> disabled student learning environment

Parts of speech are converted into other parts of speech. Verbs become nouns:

> America is on the improve.

Even more often, nouns become verbs:

> The design was prototyped into a working model.

> We're going to incentivize these people by multiyearing their program.

It appears there isn't a noun that can't be verbed!

Abstractions and empty terms disguise real meaning. Under the mistaken impression that something obscure is profound and that complexity has clout, writers stifle their natural style. They don't write "We tested it and it works," but "During the course of the above referenced investigation, data were developed and subjected to rigorous computer modeling which suggest that the system will, within specified parameters, produce viable results."

The first step in getting readers to pay attention to what we're writing is to pay attention ourselves. Too often we regurgitate phrases without having digested their meaning ("decisional significance"). We use high-sounding words for the sake of being high-sounding—or to avoid being direct.

> The income derived from the revenue enhancement program will be allocated to revitalizing the nation's infrastructure.

> **Translation:** The gasoline tax will pay for repairing our highways and sewer systems.

In jargon-laden writing, **buzz words** abound. Many are legitimate words that overuse has turned into clichés (viable, image, dialogue, disseminate, implement, relate). Some are legitimate words in certain contexts but their popular usage tends to be incorrect (parameter, modality, metaphor). Some have minimal claim to legitimacy (finalize, learning experience, out years, throughput, taxwise).

> A good catchword can obscure analysis
> for fifty years.—*Wendell L. Wilkie*

Evoke Images

Our language is rich with graphic words.

bamboo curtain	domino theory
the big bang	grass-roots campaign
bottleneck	linear thinking

These words appeal to the senses; they help the reader visualize and remember. Yet writers are sometimes unaware of the imagery they are using. Their images reveal fuzzy thinking.

> His Achilles' heel was his weak knee.

> This field of research is so virginal that no human eye has ever set foot in it. (found in a Ph.D. dissertation)

Keep your images under control. The more aware you are of the pictures words make, the better you will use them. Here's how a master does it.

> Sending men to that Army is like shoveling fleas across a barnyard—not half of them get there.—*Abraham Lincoln*

Metaphors are a technique for creating images. Unlike Lincoln's simile above, which makes a comparison using the word *like*, metaphors compare directly.

> Bureaucracy is a giant mechanism operated by pygmies. —*Honoré de Balzac*

A good metaphor is transparent; it enhances meaning without drawing attention to itself. Overusing such figures of speech diminishes their effectiveness; in small doses, they are an artful device.

> How infinite is the debt owed to metaphors
> by politicians who want to speak strongly
> but are not sure what they are going to say.
> —*Winston Churchill*

Watch Small Words

Small words, if misused, can create big problems. Check whether you have used the following small words correctly.

A, an, the. Incorrect use of the articles *a* and *the* can alter meaning. Notice the difference when *the* is omitted.

> The more specific details you provide...
> The more specific the details you provide...

The first emphasizes the quantity of specific details; the second, how specific those details are. Either could be correct, so you should choose the one that's closer to your meaning.

The beginning sound of the next word determines whether you use *a* or *an*. A consonant sound (which is not necessarily a consonant) is preceded by *a*, a vowel sound by *an*.

> a uniform, *but* an unprecedented
> a European, *but* an Easterner
> a history, *but* an hour
> a one-dollar bill, *but* an only child

Uniform and *European* are pronounced as if they began with the letter y, so *a* is the correct article to use with them. The *h* in *history* is pronounced, so it requires *a*. The *h* in *hour* is silent, calling for *an*. *One* is pronounced as if it begins with *w*, whereas the initial sound of *only* is *o*.

The choice of article to precede initials and acronyms is another trap for unwary writers. Again, it is how the word is pronounced that matters. Do you pronounce the letters individually (SEC lawyer, NBA player)? If so, do they sound as if they begin with a vowel or a consonant? "S" sounds as if it were spelled "ess" and "N" as if it were "en." With both of those acronyms, you should use *an*.

Is the acronym pronounced as a word? Then use the article *a* if it's pronounced with a consonant sound (a NATO official), or *an* if it has a vowel sound (an OSHA ruling).

Like, as. Use *like* in direct comparisons of nouns.

> Hell hath no fury like a bureaucrat scorned.—*Milton Friedman*

> Nothing recedes like success.—*Walter Winchell*

Use *as* when the comparison involves verbs.

> Do as I do.
> He resented the implication, as anyone would.

Etc. Relying on *etc.* at the end of a series of items suggests that you are either lazy or uncertain about what else to include. Indicate incompleteness by writing *such as* (or *such...as*) ahead of examples.

> A well-stocked library will include such authors as...
> The event produced additional sources of income, such as...

's. Errors of agreement with the contraction *'s* are so common that it's probably smart to scrutinize each use of the apostrophe. *It's*, *there's*, *here's*, and *that's* are ALWAYS contractions, usually of the word *is*: *it is*, *there is*, *here is*, and *that is*. The word *is* is singular. Most people know this, yet they make the mistake of treating the contraction of *is* as a plural. Though they would never write "There is three reasons," they might let "There's three reasons" slip by. Expand contractions to see if they harbor the word *is*. If they do, and you need a plural verb, use *are*. "There are three reasons."

It's is probably the most misused word in American writing. Since the apostrophe is one way to show possession, it may seem logical to use one when making the word *it* possessive. But *its* is already possessive. The only time you need to add an apostrophe is when the word is a contraction of *it is* or *it has*.

> It's a question that suggests its answer.

it's = it is or it has

Reading good writing is an excellent way to absorb the rules discussed in this chapter. How do these authors handle language? Reading the best classical and modern writers will give you more insight into ways to use words effectively than you will get from reading about good writing—and it's a lot more fun.

6 Second-Level Editing: Punctuation

> Word carpentry is like any other kind of carpentry. You must join your sentences smoothly.—*Anatole France*

Punctuation marks are road signs to help the reader: Slow down, detour, stop. Too much punctuation makes writing choppy, too little creates confusion. Its purpose is to clarify meaning, not erect roadblocks, so use it with that in mind.

Apostrophes

Apostrophes primarily show possession or a contraction; they are also used with certain plurals.

Use an apostrophe to show possession, as follows:

- With all singular words, add *'s*.

  the jury's verdict
  the twin's room (one person)
  the witness's testimony
  Jane Nelson's job

- With all plural words that end in *s*, add the apostrophe only.

  teachers' conference
  the twins' mother
  the witnesses' testimony
  the Nelsons' house

- With plural words that don't end in *s*, add *'s*.

  children's toys
  men's room
  women's issues

When you want the final *sis* or *siz* sound to be pronounced, add *'s* rather than just the apostrophe.

  Marx's philosophy

To avoid such common errors as "the Nelson's house," first make the word plural (Nelsons), then add the apostrophe to make it possessive (Nelsons').

When making a phrase or compound noun possessive, add 's to the last word.

    my brother-in-law's Lexus
    the Surgeon General's warning
    the senator from Maine's vote

However, making a phrase possessive can get out of hand.

    Poor: the officer who resigned last week's signature
    Better: the signature of the officer who resigned last week

When there is joint ownership of a single item, add 's to the last name only: Laura and Tom's car (one car). When the ownership is not joint, add 's to each name: Laura's and Tom's cars (two cars).

Apostrophes are often omitted in names of organizations, institutions or countries that end in s, where the words are more descriptive than possessive.

    Teachers College
    Consumers Union
    Publishers Weekly
    United Nations delegate

Apostrophes are usually—but not always—used in organization names that do not end in s.

    Longshoremen's Union
    McDonald's
    but Childrens Hospital *or* Children's Hospital

Find a reasonably reliable source of information about a given name (letterhead, web site, phonebook) and use that form.

Use an apostrophe to show a contraction or omission.

> can't (cannot)
> haven't (have not)
> it's (it is)
> ma'am (madam)
> o'clock (of the clock)
> Spirit of '76
> there's (there is)
> won't (will not)

> Be awful nice to 'em going up, because you're gonna meet 'em all comin' down.—*Jimmy Durante*

Note: *It's* is a contraction of *it is* or *it has*; *its* (without the apostrophe) is a possessive pronoun.

> **Contraction:** It's not the men in my life that counts—it's the life in my men.—*Mae West*

> **Possession:** There is more to life than increasing its speed. —*Mohandas K. Gandhi*

Use an apostrophe to show duration.

> one minute's delay
> two weeks' vacation
> ten years' experience

Use an apostrophe where needed for clarity and with certain plurals.

2x4's
C.O.D.'s
do's and don'ts
M.D.'s
Ph.D.'s
p's and q's

There are two c's in accumulate.
Her report card had 3 A's.

However, plurals are usually shown not by adding an apostrophe but just by adding *s* or *es*.

Don't use apostrophes in the following cases:

Wrong:	Right:
CD's	CDs
keeping up with the Jones's	keeping up with the Joneses
one's and two's	ones and twos
"The Red Pony" 's ending	the ending of "The Red Pony"
the Roaring '20's	the Roaring '20s *or* Twenties

Colons

Colons have two main jobs: to introduce something that follows, and to provide separation (as in ratios). Capitalize the first word after a colon if it begins a complete sentence.

Use a colon to introduce something.

The difference between intelligence and education is this: Intelligence will make you a good living.—*Charles F. Kettering*

The results of the survey may be summarized as follows: in favor of rezoning, 59%; opposed, 41%.

Carney's Law: There's at least a 50-50 chance that someone will print the name Craney incorrectly.—*Jim Canrey*

Use a colon to separate certain words or numbers.

Kids Write Right! (Berkeley: Tricycle Press, 2000)
Congressional Directory, Washington: U.S. Government
    Printing Office
12:30 p.m.
Matthew 6:3-7
Nature 3:127-9
Dear Ms. Fortune:
a ratio of 2:1
proportions of 5:3:1

Don't use a colon to introduce words that would fit smoothly into the sentence without the colon.

Wrong: Lewis Carroll defines arithmetic as: ambition, distraction, uglification, and derision.

Right: Lewis Carroll defines arithmetic as ambition, distraction...

Wrong: The effects of the reorganization are: an increase in productivity and a reduction in absenteeism and personnel turnover.

Right: The effects of the reorganization are an increase...

Don't use a colon when the word "follows" or "following" does not immediately precede whatever is listed.

Wrong: A list of those attending follows. Notice that management and labor are both represented:
  Jack Johnson
  Laurel Ann Schmidt
  Robin Reynolds

Right: A list of those attending follows. Notice that management and labor are both represented.
  Jack Johnson
  Laurel Ann Schmidt
  Robin Reynolds

Commas

Commas prevent misreading and clarify meaning. However, unnecessary commas are a distraction, so add only those that promote ease of reading.

Use a comma in the following:

• In compound sentences, to separate independent clauses

  I did not attend his funeral, but I wrote a nice letter saying I approved it.—*Mark Twain*

  Opportunities are usually disguised as hard work, so most people don't recognize them.—*Ann Landers*

- With nonrestrictive clauses

  The law, in its majestic equality, forbids the rich as well as the poor to sleep under bridges.—*Anatole France*

- Following participial phrases

  Thrusting my nose firmly between his teeth, I threw him heavily to the ground on top of me.—*Mark Twain*

- To indicate a pause or break in continuity

  A bore is a man who, when you ask him how he is, tells you. —*Bert Taylor*

- When addressing someone directly

  Depend upon it, sir, when a man knows he is to be hanged in a fortnight, it concentrates his mind wonderfully.—*Samuel Johnson*

- With appositives

  George Bernard Shaw, the Irish-born playwright and social critic, thought the lack of money was the root of all evil.

- With coordinate adjectives

  a tall, stately redwood
  the slow, relentless pace

  I found him a plausible, attractive rogue, all nervous energy and wit.—*Thomas Flanagan*

- With complementary or contrasting elements

  Skepticism, like chastity, should not be relinquished too readily.—*George Santayana*

  Grub first, then ethics.—*Bertolt Brecht*

- Following introductory phrases

  In the main, opera in English is just about as sensible as baseball in Italian.—*H. L. Mencken*

- In a series

  Talk low, talk slow, and don't say too much.—*John Wayne*

Note: Some consider the final comma in a series to be optional. However, by always adding the final comma, you avoid potential confusion.

  Unclear: Two developments will affect pregnancy, birth and infants.

  Clear: Two developments will affect pregnancy, birth, and infants.

- For clarity

  Even though I was young when she told me that, I understood her meaning perfectly.

  Everybody is ignorant, only on different subjects.—*Will Rogers*

  If she chooses, Adams can apply for an extension.

- With identical words or unrelated numbers

   If such a tragedy had happened to you, you would understand.

   No matter how thin you slice it, it's still baloney.—*Alfred E. Smith*

   Total enrollment is 24, 15 of whom hold advanced degrees.

- To show omission

   You are apprehensive of monarchy; I, of aristocracy.—*John Adams*

- With quotations

   Billy Rose said, "Never invest your money in anything that eats or needs repairing."

   "My goose," the chef said, "is cooked."

- When the modifier follows the modified

   The shareholders' meeting, upbeat and constructive, lasted four hours.

- With titles

   Warren Williams, Jr.
   Drew Hoffmann, Attorney at Law
   Stephanie Peabody, M.D.
   Justin Adams, Management Consultant

- Following opening subordinate clauses

   If all economists were laid end to end, they would not reach a conclusion.—*George Bernard Shaw*

- With parenthetical expressions

  It requires an unusual mind, according to Alfred North Whitehead, to analyze the obvious.

  Prophecy, however honest, is generally a poor substitute for experience.—*Justice Benjamin N. Cardozo*

Don't use commas in the following cases:

- Between short, closely related clauses

  Some carve great careers while others simply chisel.
  —*Laurence J. Peter*

- Between an independent and a dependent clause

  <u>Finance is the art of passing currency from hand</u>
  independent clause
  <u>to hand</u> <u>until it finally disappears.</u>—*Robert Sarnoff*
  ....dependent clause

  Don't talk unless you can improve the silence.—*Vermont proverb*

- With restrictive clauses

  Men <u>who have a pierced ear</u> are better prepared
  ....restrictive clause
  for marriage; they buy jewelry and they've experienced pain.—*Rita Rudner*

  An optimist is a driver who thinks that an empty space at the curb won't have a fire hydrant beside it.

- Following the last item in a series

  His reports occasionally lapse into disorganized, incoherent, jargon-filled writing. (*not* jargon-filled, writing)

- Between adjectives where the first modifies both the second adjective and the noun

  illegal campaign contributions
  a snowy Christmas eve

Dashes

Dashes are an interruption, like waving your finger under the reader's nose. Whenever a colon, semicolon, or comma would serve just as well, use it. Reserve the dash for situations where dramatic emphasis is justified.

Use a dash in the following cases:

- To emphasize what follows

  Familiarity breeds contempt—and children.—*Mark Twain*

  When I was six I made my mother a little hat—out of her new blouse.—*Lilly Daché*

- To indicate an abrupt change or an afterthought

  The business of government is to keep the government out of business—that is, unless business needs government aid. —*Will Rogers*

  The best way to keep children home is to make the home atmosphere pleasant—and let the air out of the tires.— *Dorothy Parker*

- To summarize or explain

  The principle of give and take is the principle of diplomacy—give one and take ten.—*Mark Twain*

> A pedestrian is a man who has two cars—one being driven by his wife, the other by one of his children.—*Robert Benchley*

Dashes can be combined with exclamation marks, question marks, and quotation marks.

> Her response was emphatic—"I will not sign this!"

But don't combine one dash with a comma.

> **Wrong:** The books—all 12 of them, were overdue.

> **Right:** The books—all 12 of them—were overdue.

Word processors provide both an em dash (—) and an en dash (–). The above examples call for an em dash. The en dash is primarily used to indicate inclusiveness.

> 1988–89
> pp. 35–47
> New York–Boston train

A 2-em dash indicates omitted letters (Ms. T——, D——d right!). A 3-em dash replaces entire words, as in a bibliography where it is used instead of repeating an author's name.

On a standard typewriter keyboard, use two hyphens for an em dash and one hyphen for an en dash.

Exclamation Points

Exclamation points provide a punchy ending. Use exclamation points after interjections:

> Ouch!

after exclamatory sentences:

> That hurt!

and after imperative sentences that indicate strong feelings:

> Don't step on my toe again!

Too many exclamation points leave a reader feeling punched out, so save them for just a few important places.

Hyphens

Hyphens divide words at the end of the line (see Word Division, p. 162) and join certain words to form compounds (break-in, old-fashioned music).

Hyphenate a few prefixes.

anti-hero
ex-husband
post-mortem

Today, most prefixes are not hyphenated.

bipartisan
infrastructure
interrelated
macroeconomics
microorganism
millisecond
multitasking
nanotechnology
preempt
reenter
semiconductor

However, retain the hyphen in the following cases:

• When confusion or an awkward pronunciation results from the one-word form

co-owner
re-read
co-opt
un-ionized
co-worker

• When the root word is capitalized

sub-Saharan
pro-Israeli

pre-Columbian
post-World War I

- When the second part of a hyphenated term consists of two or more words

  non-tumor-bearing tissue
  post-20th-century inventions
  pre-gold-strike era
  ultra-high-speed device

- When certain double or triple letters would occur

  anti-intellectual
  non-native
  semi-independent
  shell-like

Hyphenate fractions and compound numbers.

  one-third
  forty-seven

Hyphenate to combine a numeral and noun or adjective (a unit modifier).

  $^1/_2$-acre lot
  10-kilometer run
  5-ml beaker
  50-odd members
  75-page report

Hyphenate certain compounds.
Your meaning determines whether to hyphenate a compound

word. An *old film buff* describes an elderly person who enjoys movies. An *old-film buff* is someone who enjoys old films.

Hyphenate to prevent misreading in such cases as the following.

Adjectives

> bricks-and-mortar bookstore
> dog-eared book
> double-decker bus
> economy-sized package
> fast-talking salesperson
> good-natured response
> in-house memo
> just-in-time inventory
> long-term effects
> revolving-door policy
> stiff-necked attitude
> thought-provoking statement
> time-honored custom

> The best mind-altering drug is truth.—*Lily Tomlin*

> Brevity is only skin deep, and the world is full of thin-skinned people.—*Richard Armour*

Nouns

> break-in
> go-between
> know-how
> ne'er-do-well
> page-turner

poet-humorist
well-wisher
write-off

There are no whole truths; all truths are half-truths.—*Alfred North Whitehead*

Improvised Compounds

dog-eat-dog
do-it-yourself
Johnny-come-lately
stick-to-itiveness
topsy-turvy
touch-me-not

Nowadays people are divided into three classes—the Haves, the Have-nots, and the Have-Not-Paid-for-What-They-Haves.—*Earl Wilson*

Omit hyphens in established compounds when they are not needed to clarify meaning.

city hall news
high school dropout
real estate office
White House staff

See p. 172 for a more complete discussion of the formation of compound words.

Don't use hyphens in the following cases:

antiwar
bilateral

catlike
coordinate
midtown
overanxious
postdoctoral
statewide
transcontinental
underfunded

Never hyphenate a word ending in *-ly*.

Wrong: widely-known author, commonly-held assumption, publicly-held stock

Right: widely known author, commonly held assumption, publicly held stock

Parentheses

Parentheses have the effect of an aside, as if you were trying to say the words behind your hand. Use them only now and then or your writing will lack directness.

Use parentheses to set off an explanation or to add information.

The teacher (who chose not to reveal his identity) submitted a list of the crazy excuses he'd received for late homework.

When the parentheses contain a complete statement or question, put the closing punctuation mark inside the final parenthesis.

(She is the shortstop.)
(Was he dreaming?)

Periods

Periods are used at the ends of sentences and abbreviations. In the UK, the period is called a "full stop," which is a good description of what it does.

Use a period as follows:

- At the end of a declarative sentence (a statement)

  Artificial intelligence is no match for natural stupidity.

- At the end of an imperative sentence (instructions, requests, orders)

  Get your facts first. Then you can distort them as you please.—*Mark Twain*

- With some abbreviations and initials

  p.m.
  Mr./Ms./Mrs.
  vs.
  etc.
  J. F. Kennedy, *but* JFK (no periods)

If an abbreviation ends a sentence, don't add a second period.

  We will expect you at 10 a.m.

An *ellipsis* consists of three periods. It is used to show an omission within quoted material.

  A great many people have...asked how I manage to get so much work done and still keep looking so dissipated. —*Robert Benchley*

If the ellipsis *follows* the period that ends a sentence, put a space between that period and the ellipses.

> The only way to get rid of temptation is to yield to it. ...I can resist everything but temptation.—*Oscar Wilde*

If the ellipsis *precedes* the period that ends a sentence, use four evenly spaced periods.

> An important scientific innovation rarely makes its way by gradually winning over and converting its opponents.... What does happen is that its opponents gradually die out.
> —*Max Planck*

Question Marks

Put a question mark after a direct question (in other words, at the end of an interrogative sentence).

> Did you check out the web site?
> Who is preparing the report?

Do not use a question mark with an indirect question or polite request.

> He asked who is making the reservation.
> Will you please close the door as you leave.

Quotation Marks

Quotation marks have several jobs.

• To enclose titles of short pieces (songs, poems, articles, short stories)

> Do you know the words to "The Star-Spangled Banner"?

- To set words or phrases apart from the surrounding text

  When the government talks about "raising capital," it means printing it.—*Peter Drucker*

  The package was marked "Refused—Return to Sender."

  I prefer the word "homemaker" because "housewife" implies that there may be a wife someplace else.—*Bella Abzug*

  The bride and groom said their "I do's."

- As a substitute for the words *so-called*

  The "error" identified by the grammar-checker was actually correct.

- To indicate spoken words

  Victor Borge said, "Laughter is the shortest distance between two people."

  Diplomacy is the art of saying "Nice doggie!" till you can find a rock.—*Wynn Catlin*

Single quotation marks enclose quoted material within a quotation.

  Richard Armour quipped, "That money talks I'll not deny. I heard it once: It said, 'Goodbye.'"

  Kin Hubbard asked, "Why don't th' feller who says, 'I'm not a speechmaker,' let it go at that instead of giving a demonstration?"

Punctuate quoted material as follows:

- Place periods and commas inside the closing quotation mark.

  "Money won't buy happiness," according to Bill Vaughan, "but it will pay the salaries of a large research staff to study the problem."

- Place all other punctuation marks outside the closing quotation mark, unless they are part of what is quoted.

  He shouted, "May Day! May Day!"

  Did you hear them calling "Help"?

  Thoreau asked the question, "What is the use of a house if you haven't got a tolerable planet to put it on?"

Semicolons

The semicolon produces a more emphatic break than a comma. Use semicolons when you want a stronger pause than a comma but less separation than two sentences.

Use a semicolon between independent clauses.

Beware of little expenses; a small leak will sink a great ship. —*Benjamin Franklin*

The brain is a wonderful organ; it starts working the moment you get up in the morning and doesn't stop until you get to the office.—*Robert Frost*

Hanging is too good for a man who makes puns; he should be drawn and quoted.—*Fred Allen*

One friend in a lifetime is much; two are many; three are hardly possible.—*Henry Adams*

I'm not a vegetarian because I love animals; I'm a vegetarian because I hate plants.—*A. Whitney Brown*

Use a semicolon between items in a series that contains commas.

> If a man runs after money, he's money-mad; if he keeps it, he's a capitalist; if he spends it, he's a playboy; if he doesn't get it, he's a ne'er-do-well; if he doesn't try to get it, he lacks ambition. If he gets it without working for it, he's a parasite; and if he accumulates it after a lifetime of hard work, people call him a fool who never got anything out of life.
> —*Vic Oliver*

Don't use a semicolon between an independent clause and a dependent (or subordinate) clause.

> **Wrong:** The project will not be funded; even though it is worthwhile.

> **Right:** The project will not be funded even though it is worthwhile.

7 Second-Level Editing: Grammar

> Grammar, rhetoric, and logic enrich
> enormously the phenomenon of
> being alive.—*George Santayana*

Good grammar is transparent. Instead of getting in the way, it helps readers understand what is written.

Most people use grammatical rules without being aware of them. But occasionally a question comes up: Should a verb be singular or plural? Which pronoun should I use: *I, me,* or *myself; who* or *whom*? Knowing the rules (or where to find them) answers such questions.

This section covers the six areas where most grammatical questions arise: agreement, pronouns, adjectives and adverbs, verbs, parallel structure, and no-fault sentences. Use these guidelines to sharpen your awareness of potential problems. The examples and rules will help you detect and correct errors.

Agreement
Every part of a sentence should agree with every related part. If you translate this rule into everyday English, you find it's saying something like this:

- Use singular verbs with singular subjects and plural verbs with plural subjects.

- Make a pronoun singular if its antecedent is singular and plural if the antecedent is plural.

Let's look at those two areas: subject/verb and antecedent/pronoun.

Make subject and verb agree in number.

A singular subject requires a singular verb.

> The wastepaper <u>basket</u> <u>is</u> a writer's best friend.
>   sing.   sing.
>   subj.   verb
> —*Isaac Bashevis Singer*

A plural subject requires a plural verb.

> **We are confronted** with insurmountable opportunities.
> pl. subj. pl. verb
> *—Pogo (Walt Kelly)*

The verb must also agree with the subject when the subject follows the verb.

> What are the answers?
> There is one doctor.
> Answering questions from the press were three candidates.
>
> Behind the phony tinsel of Hollywood lies the real tinsel.
> *—Oscar Levant*

A compound subject joined by *and* requires a plural verb (a compound subject consists of two or more elements).

> **The rich man and his daughter are** soon parted.
> compound subject   pl. verb
> *—Kin Hubbard*
>
> Completing the form and mailing it promptly are both important.
>
> Only presidents, editors, and people with tapeworms have the right to use the editorial "we."*—Mark Twain*

A compound subject joined by *or* or *nor* takes a singular verb.

> A passport or tourist card is necessary.

If a compound subject is treated as a unit, it takes a singular verb.

Find and Replace is a useful word-processing function.
Baxter & Grand is a national accounting firm.

A compound subject preceded by the word *each* or *every* is singular.

Each question and answer was carefully considered.
Every representative and senator is on our mailing list.

When *as well as* precedes a word or phrase, it does not affect the number of the verb.

The owner, as well as his employees, is implicated.

In *either/or* and *neither/nor* constructions, the verb agrees with the nearest noun.

Either the equipment or the <u>samples</u> <u>were</u> contaminated.
plural subj. plural verb

Neither envelopes nor <u>letterhead</u> <u>was</u> delivered.
sing. subj.   sing. verb

The number of the verb is not affected by intervening phrases.

Working conditions, a subject of frequent debate, are...
The briefcase with the missing reports is...
The verb in the main clause of each of these examples is...
The verbs in each sentence are...
One in every ten components is...

Treat the following indefinite pronouns as singular: each, each one, every, everyone, everybody, either, neither, nobody, no one, any, anyone, anybody, somebody, someone.

In the United States there is more space where nobody is than where anybody is.—*Gertrude Stein*

However, when *each* follows a plural subject, the verb is plural.

The teachers each have different ideas for solving the problem.

Treat the following indefinite pronouns either as singular or plural, depending on the context or meaning: none, some, more, all, most, half.

All's fair in love and war.—*Francis Edward Smedley*

All want to be learned, but none is willing to pay the price. —*Juvenal*

More is experienced in one day in the life of a learned man than in the whole lifetime of an ignorant man.—*Seneca*

More are experienced programmers than in previous years.

The word *number* is singular when preceded by *the*, plural when preceded by *a*.

The number of mistakes was small.
A number of mistakes were made.

Collective nouns (such as family, group, committee, couple, team, personnel, staff, majority) are singular unless they refer to individuals within the group.

The personnel were screened for verbal and mathematical aptitudes. *(Individuals within the group were screened.)*

The team was late. *(The group is treated as a unit.)*

The contents of the test tube was withdrawn. *(as a whole)*

The contents of the package were examined. *(as individual elements)*

A subject that expresses a sum, rate, measurement, or quantity as a unit takes a singular verb even if the subject is plural.

Three centimeters is more than one inch.
Five dollars is a reasonable price.

Some words ending in *s* appear to be plural but are actually a singular concept: news, physics, economics, series, summons.

The news is good.
The series of tests was completed.

Handle relative pronouns (*who, which, that, what*) as follows:

- *Who, which,* and *that* take singular verbs when referring to singular words, plural verbs when referring to plural words.

  Singular: Anyone who hates children and dogs can't be all bad.—*W. C. Fields*

  Plural: People who bite the hand that feeds them usually lick the boot that kicks them.—*Eric Hoffer*

- *What* takes a singular verb, unless it has a plural antecedent.

  What kills a skunk is the publicity it gives itself.—*Abraham Lincoln*

Agreement should be between verb and subject, not between verb and complement.

The <u>solution</u> <u>is</u> <u>strong locks.</u>
subject   verb   complement

When the subject is a phrase or clause, use a singular verb.

> **Freedom of the press** is limited to those who own one.
> subject
> —*A. J. Liebling*

Certain Latin words are the source of errors of agreement (*phenomena, criteria*). The table on p. 73 shows which words have retained their Latin plurals and which have been Anglicized.

Make pronoun and antecedent agree in number.

> All <u>employees</u> must provide <u>their</u> own tools.

> He is a self-made <u>man</u> and worships <u>his</u> creator.—*William Cowper*

> Whatever <u>women</u> do <u>they</u> must do twice as well as men to be thought half as good. Luckily, this is not difficult. —*Charlotte Whitton*

> When the <u>jury</u> returns to give <u>its</u> verdict...

> Neither <u>Karen</u> nor <u>Linda</u> would break <u>her</u> silence. (Compounds joined by *or* or *nor* are singular.)

> <u>Men</u> are never so tired and harassed as when <u>they</u> have to deal with a woman who wants a raise.—*Michael Korda*

> The <u>tongue</u> weighs almost nothing, yet few people can hold <u>it</u>.

Pronouns
Use the correct case of pronouns.

Nominative	Possessive	Objective
I	my	me
you	your, yours	you
he	his	him
she	her, hers	her
it	its	it
we	our, ours	us
they	their, theirs	them
who	whose	whom

Use the nominative case when the pronoun is the subject.

> People <u>who</u> say <u>they</u> sleep like a baby usually don't have one.—*Leo Burke*
> (*Who* is the subject of the verb *say; they* is the subject of the verb *sleep.*)

> Wilson and I will attend.

Use the objective case when the pronoun is the object of a verb or preposition.

> Marriage is the alliance of two people, one of <u>whom</u> never remembers birthdays and the other never forgets <u>them</u>. —*Ogden Nash*
> (*Whom* is the object of the preposition *of; them* is the object of the verb *forgets.*)

> Submit the report to Wilson and me.

Use the possessive case when you want to show ownership.

> I should have the courage of my lack of conviction.—*Tom Stoppard*

> Wilson and Gaines missed their flight.

Once you've determined the correct case, you know which pronoun to use (for example, *I* or *me*, *who* or *whom*). The choice is easier if you mentally eliminate everything between the verb or preposition and the pronoun whose case you're trying to determine. Try it in the following example.

Wrong: The contest has narrowed down to [you and] I.

Right: The contest has narrowed down to you and me.

When in doubt about *who* or *whom*, substitute a pronoun for the word. If a nominative pronoun feels right (*I, we, she*), use *who* (the nominative form of the word). If an objective

pronoun fits (*me*, *us*, *her*), use *whom* (the objective form of the word).

> The first person who answers all questions correctly... (*she* answers all questions...)

> The woman whom we hired has an MBA. (we hired *her*)

Even though the word *whoever* follows the preposition *for* in the following example, its role as subject of the verb *had* in the dependent clause "whoever had jobs" determines the case.

> **Wrong:** They worked for whomever had jobs.

> **Right:** They worked for whoever had jobs.

If a pronoun follows *than* or *as*, mentally insert the missing verbs to determine the correct case. (The missing words are in parentheses in the following examples.)

> I am as hard-working as he (is).

> The supervisor corrects Smith more often than (she corrects) me.

> The supervisor corrects Smith more often than I (do).

Avoid unnecessary reflexive or intensive pronouns (pronouns ending in *-self* or *-selves*).

> **Wrong:** The summons was received by my partner and myself.
> **Right:** The summons was received by my partner and me.

> **Wrong:** My partner and myself received...
> **Right:** My partner and I received...

A reflexive pronoun is correctly used only when it refers back to the subject (*He injured himself*), and an intensive pronoun is used strictly for emphasis (*I will present the award myself*).

Make pronouns refer clearly to their antecedents.

A pronoun is a stand-in; the word or group of words it stands in for is called its antecedent. A reader should have no doubt about what antecedent a pronoun replaces.

<u>Celeste</u> gave the valet <u>her</u> car keys.
antecedent   pronoun

Ambiguous pronouns create confusion.

Unclear: She told her that her secretary had typed her resignation. *(Whose secretary? Whose resignation?)*

Unclear: Company A is losing sales to Company B and its competitors. *(Whose competitors, A's or B's?)*

Sometimes the antecedent is missing entirely.

Unclear: When you calculate the number of managers and subordinates, <u>it</u> is eye-opening. *(What does it refer to? Probably the ratio of managers to subordinates, which appears in the sentence only indirectly.)*

Clear: When you calculate the number of managers and subordinates, the ratio is eye-opening.

Adjectives and Adverbs

Use adjectives to modify nouns or pronouns; use adverbs to modify verbs, adjectives, or other adverbs.

The following examples illustrate correct usage.

> She gave a <u>quick</u> answer. *(adj., modifies the noun **answer**; it describes what kind of answer)*

> She answered <u>quickly.</u> *(adv., modifies the verb **answer**; it tells how she answered)*

> a <u>public</u> company *(adj., modifies the noun company)*

> a <u>publicly</u> held company *(adv., modifies the adjective **held**)*

> The reporter was <u>uncertain.</u> *(adj., modifies **reporter**)*

> The reporter answered <u>uncertainly.</u> *(adv., modifies **answered**)*

> I feel <u>bad</u> about the mix-up. *(adj., modifies the pronoun **I**)*

> I feel <u>badly</u> treated. *(adv., modifies the verb **treated**)*

Put modifiers where they will produce the desired meaning.

> **Wrong:** Children are sometimes placed in Juvenile Hall because there are inadequate foster homes to meet their needs.
>
> **Right:** Children are sometimes placed in Juvenile Hall because of an inadequate supply of foster homes.

> **Wrong:** This page was left intentionally blank.
> **Right:** This page was intentionally left blank.

Have you chosen the best modifier for the job?

> **Wrong:** The chemical dissolves readily and only a small dose can be fatal.

A large dose cannot? Replacing *only* with *even* makes it a sensible sentence.

In general, place modifiers close to the words they modify. **Misplaced modifiers** are often ambiguous or unintentionally funny.

> The patient has had chest pain when she lies on her left side for over a year.

> The chimpanzees were observed using binoculars.

> Staff members should submit a completed travel voucher with the required receipts attached to their department heads.

Dangling modifiers are another common error of placement. A dangler usually begins the sentence; what it modifies has been omitted.

> Checking the records, the error was found.

Since "the error" cannot have been "checking the records," the opening phrase is left dangling. Add the correct subject to the main clause to remedy the situation.

> Checking the records, Analisa found the error.

Here are some other dangling modifiers. Watch for such illogical constructions and rewrite to include the correct subject.

> **Dangler:** Walking along the tracks, the train whistled in the distance.
> **Correct:** Walking along the tracks, I heard the train whistle in the distance.

> **Dangler:** Having read the instructions carefully, my bicycle was easily assembled.
> **Correct:** Having read the instructions carefully, I was able to assemble my bicycle easily.

> **Dangler:** On arriving at the third floor, her apartment is the first door on the left.
> **Correct:** On arriving at the third floor, you will find her apartment is the first door on the left.

Not all dangling modifiers are as easy to detect as they are in the above examples. I found a more subtle dangler in the following sentence from a letter to shareholders. As written, the person writing the letter will be the one receiving the monthly dividends! The sentence breaks several other good-writing rules as well: It's pompous, wordy, too long, and uses the passive voice.

> In addition to receiving a monthly dividend, we believe this transaction to be beneficial to you because it allows you to participate more directly in the ongoing opportunities presented by deregulation and consolidation in the utility industry.

Here's my slimmed-down and corrected version:

> Your investment will not only continue to pay monthly dividends but will be part of the business opportunities that follow as regulations change and companies merge in the utility industry.

Verbs
Use the correct verb tense.
The correct tense comes naturally to most native-born writers. A tense that sounds right probably is right.

Present:	I walk
Past:	I walked
Future:	I will walk
Present Perfect:	I have walked (an action that began in the past and continues or is completed in the present)
Past Perfect:	I had walked (an action that began and was completed in the past)

| Future Perfect: | I will have walked (an action that will begin in the future and be completed by a specific time) |

Yesterday I was a dog. Today I'm a dog. Tomorrow I'll probably still be a dog. Sigh. There's so little hope for advancement.—*Snoopy (Charles Schulz)*

Where problems usually arise is in maintaining logical consistency. If you have chosen the present tense to describe a marketing study ("Our survey shows..."), use the present tense throughout ("that both men and women prefer..."). Especially when editing a long document, read it once just to check whether you have used tenses logically and consistently.

Here are two examples where decisions about verb tense are needed.

He <u>wondered</u> whether the system (is) (was) fair.
    past tense

Next, the manager <u>explains</u> how the system (works)
              present tense
(worked).

In these examples, the tense of the first verbs (*wondered, explains*) dictates the tense of verbs that follow. Thus, *was* and *works* are the correct choices.

An exception is a statement of "universal truth" which calls for the present tense even when the main verb is in the past tense.

Newton <u>discovered</u> that apples <u>fall.</u>
          past tense   present tense

Benjamin Franklin <u>knew</u> that creditors <u>have</u> better
                        past tense   present tense
memories than debtors.

The first verb in each of the following examples is in the perfect tense. What is the correct tense for subsequent verbs? (The choices are shown in parentheses.)

They would have liked (to be) (to have been) the winners.
Johnson has enjoyed (being) (having been) governor.
It would have been easy for the department (to change) (to have changed) the procedure.

Piling up perfect tenses has an almost tongue-twisting effect (e.g., *would have liked to have been*). Logic suggests that you should keep subsequent verbs in the present tense, unless their action precedes the main verb. Correct choices in these examples are as follows:

They would have liked to be the winners.
Johnson has enjoyed being governor.
It would have been easy for the department to change the procedure.

Use the correct mood.
Most of our sentences are in the indicative mood.

Invention is the mother of necessity.—*Thorstein Veblen*

The interrogative mood asks a question.

> I am responsible for my actions, but who is responsible for General Motors?—*Ralph Nader*

Commands and most instructions are in the imperative mood.

> Press the red lever.

The following examples illustrate the few uses of the subjunctive mood in today's writing:

- An improbable condition or one that is contrary to fact

  > If I <u>were</u> younger, I would challenge you to a match.

- An indirect command

  > She specified that the money <u>be</u> donated to charity.
  > His friend insisted that he <u>drive</u> the car.

- Motions and resolutions

  > I move that the motion <u>be</u> adopted.
  > Resolved, That the question <u>be submitted</u> to the full membership.

Shall or Will? The traditional distinction between *shall* and *will* has all but disappeared. *Will* has generally replaced *shall* in all future tenses. *Shall* still appears in some government and legal writing, where it probably results from the mistaken belief that *shall* sounds more authoritative.

> **Stilted:** The contractor shall provide all the necessary materials.

> **Natural:** The contractor will provide all the necessary materials.

Parallel Structure

Make related parts of a sentence or heading parallel in form.

This helps readers grasp the connection between the parallel elements and thus helps them understand your meaning. Aesthetics and dramatic effect are also enhanced. "Give me liberty or kill me" wouldn't have gone far in stirring patriotism.

To create parallel structure, make an infinitive parallel with an infinitive, an adjective with an adjective, and so on. In the following example, a series of active verbs is followed, unnecessarily, by a passive verb.

> Unparallel: At the meeting we will (1) discuss the proposed ordinance, (2) listen to citizen comments, (3) take a vote, and (4) the meeting will then be adjourned.
>
> Parallel: At the meeting we will (1) discuss the proposed ordinance, (2) listen to citizen comments, (3) take a vote, and (4) adjourn.

> Unparallel: A moment not only of suspense but excitement...
>
> Parallel: A moment not only of suspense but of excitement...

> Unparallel: The description was both accurate and it was easy to read.
>
> Parallel: The description was both accurate and readable.

No-Fault Sentences

Grammarians love fancy terms. Case in point: **sentence faults.** These in turn are identified as **fragments** and **run-ons.** A run-on is further described as a **fused sentence** and a **comma**

splice. Though a fragment is occasionally useful, a run-on is always against the rules. Let's go into the whys and wherefores.

Use fragments with care.

A *fragment* is a partial sentence; it may lack a subject or predicate, and it does not express a complete thought. The *Dictionary of Modern English Usage* calls fragments "verbless sentences" that enliven writing by making it more like spoken language. Fragments are appropriate in dialogue or in a question-and-answer format.

> Will they win? Not if we can help it.

Use fragments sparingly for emphasis or to achieve a particular effect.

> Our guarantee is good for one year. Without exception.

Avoid fragments in formal writing. If you have trouble detecting fragments, study the following examples.

> **Fragment:** Knowing that the meeting would be disrupted if she arrived late.
> **Complete:** Knowing that the meeting would be disrupted if she arrived late, she was careful to be on time.

> **Fragment:** Long but incomplete thoughts that masquerade, right up to the end, as complete thoughts.
> **Complete:** Watch out for long but incomplete thoughts that masquerade, right up to the end, as complete thoughts.

> **Fragment:** When I think I know all the answers.
> **Complete:** When I think I know all the answers, life asks some more questions.

Avoid run-ons.

Run-ons are two independent clauses joined only by a comma (a *comma splice*) or by no punctuation (a *fused sentence*). If the clauses are closely related, rewrite run-ons by joining the clauses with a semicolon. But if you want a stronger break, separate a run-on into two sentences.

> **Run-on:** I had another flying lesson today I learned how to stall the plane.

> **Correct:** I had another flying lesson today; I learned how to stall the plane.

Run-ons with the word *however* are especially common.

> **Run-on:** We had planned to move into the new building in May, however, construction delays forced us to change our plans.

> **Correct:** We had planned to move into the new building in May. However, construction delays...

8 Second-Level Editing: Mechanical Style

> Each communication is a challenge to the writer to present information and ideas directly and forcefully, to help the reader along, and to affect the reader in a chosen way.—*Robert Barrass*

When you edit for mechanical style, you check such matters as spelling, capitalization, abbreviations, and word division. You also review numbers (should they be words or figures?) and document appearance and integrity (are tables missing? are there gaps in page numbers?). These elements of style distinguish a polished document from a flawed one.

A style sheet will help you keep track of the choices you have made: capitalization (Co-Prosperity Spheres), hyphenation (non-aligned nations), number treatment (three million or 3 million), spellings (catalog or catalogue). The rules and tables in this section will help you put the finishing touches on your writing; a style sheet will make sure that you've been consistent. (How to make a style sheet is covered on p. 23).

Abbreviations

Abbreviations are seldom appropriate in formal business writing or general writing such as fiction, history, or news. They suggest that you have sloppy writing habits or were too hurried to complete the words. But some words are always abbreviated (for example, *Mr.*), and certain abbreviations are acceptable if space is tight or they avoid cumbersome repetition.

Abbreviations are acceptable in footnotes, tables, lists, and bibliographies. Technical writing also makes heavy use of them. (Technical writers should refer to a style guide for their particular discipline for the final word on abbreviations.) The following paragraphs present rules for abbreviation in business writing and in writing for publication.

In general, give the full name or term the first time it appears, followed by the abbreviated version in parentheses. Then use only the abbreviation throughout the remainder of the document.

The trend is away from the use of periods, especially with units of measurement (lb, km) and with abbreviations consisting entirely of capital letters (IRS, FDR). However, periods can be used if needed to prevent confusion when the abbreviated form spells a word (in., No.). Do not use periods with acronyms (NASA, URL) or with shortened forms of words (typo, stereo, the Fed, co-op, fax, caps).

To make an abbreviation or acronym plural, add a lowercase *s*.

   IQs
   MVPs

If the abbreviation has periods, add 's.

   Ph.D.'s

Do not begin a sentence with a symbol or abbreviation other than a social title (Ms., Dr., Mrs.).

Correct: Dr. Singh will be retiring in May.

Wrong: No. 5 shaft was the scene of the cave-in.
Correct: Number 5 shaft was the scene of the cave-in.
Better: The cave-in occurred in the No. 5 shaft.

Names and Titles

Ms.	Messrs.	Sr.	Ph.D.	M.P.
Mrs.	Mmes.	Esq.	M.A.	D.V.M.
Mr.	Jr.	M.D.	J.D.	

Note: Abbreviations are acceptable in captions (e.g., Dist. Atty. Shirley Ramos, Sen. Phil Bingham).

WRONG:	RIGHT:
Hon. Sawyer	the Honorable Deborah Sawyer, Hon. Deborah Sawyer
Rev. Angell	the Reverend Henry Angell, Rev. Henry Angell
Gen. Brook	General Brook, Gen. Donald E. Brook
Sen. Bingham	Senator Bingham, Senator Phil Bingham
D.A. Ramos	District Attorney Shirley Ramos
Dr. Samuel Stevens, M.D.	Samuel Stevens, M.D.
Mr. Owen Mills, Esq.	Owen Mills, Esq.
Professor Janice Young, Ph.D.	Janice Young, Ph.D. *or* Professor Janice Young

Agencies and Organizations

AAAS	ILGWU
AFL-CIO	IOOF
CAB	NFL
CBS	SAE
FDA	SBA

Write out company names without abbreviations in straight text (Union Pacific Railway), unless the company is known primarily by its abbreviated form (IBM).

The words *Inc.* and *Ltd.* are usually dropped. Use a firm's letterhead as a guide to the preferred abbreviated form for such terms as Brothers (Bros.), Company (Co.), and (&), Corporation (Corp.), and Incorporated (Inc.).

If space is limited, abbreviate the following in addresses:

Agency (Agcy.)
Department (Dept.)
Division (Div.)
Headquarters (Hdqrs. or HQ)
Institute (Inst.)
Subsidiary (Subs.)

Geographical Terms

N E S W   NE SE SW NW   ENE SSW NNE
   E by SE   N by NW
St. Louis, St. Paul, *but* Fort Worth, Port Arthur, Mount
   Vernon
UK, UAR *or* U.K., U.A.R.
U.S. Department of Agriculture, U.S.S. Enterprise, U.S.
   Circuit Court

Abbreviate *United States* only when it is an adjective.

> He was glad to return to the United States.

> They felt that <u>U.S.</u> foreign policy was misguided.
> adjective

Use two capital letters *with no period* to abbreviate states in mailing addresses: AL, CO, MA (*not* AL., CO.). You may use traditional state abbreviations (Colo., Mass.) in captions or footnotes, but do not abbreviate state names in text.

Dates and Times

> Jan., Feb., Mar., Apr., May, June, July, Aug., Sept., Oct., Nov., Dec.
> *or* Ja, F, Mr, Ap, My, Je, Jl, Au, S, O, N, D
> Mon., Tues., Wed., Thurs., Fri., Sat., Sun.
> sec   min   hr (or h)   da (or d)   wk   mo   yr
> a.m. *or* A.M. (*ante meridiem*)
> p.m. *or* P.M. (*post meridiem*)
> M. (noon, *meridies*)

Parts of Books or Documents

Abbreviate references to parts of books or documents only when they appear in parentheses: (Chap. 4) or (Par. 9a).

Constitutions and Bylaws

Spell out *Section* and *Article* the first time; abbreviate them thereafter.

> SECTION 1, ARTICLE 1
> SEC. 2, ART. 2

If you are uncertain about the correct abbreviation of a term, consult a good dictionary.

Capitalization

Capital letters make a word stand out. The words we capitalize reveal what we think is important or deserves emphasis. However, not everyone agrees on what is important. I have drawn on modern authorities for the following guidelines, but I've tempered them with a few prejudices of my own.

An example is the word *federal*. Some manuals specify lowercase, unless the word is part of a proper name (Federal Trade Commission). Others capitalize *federal* everywhere (Federal government, Federal agencies). I prefer lowercase, but as long as you are consistent, you have considerable latitude in such gray areas.

First Words

Capitalize the first word of a sentence.

> A hospital should also have a recovery room adjoining the cashier's office.—*Francis O'Walsh*

> Should the employees be notified? Which ones? How?

Capitalize the first word of a quotation.

> "Life is what happens when you are busy making other plans." (John Lennon)

> "The cost of living has gone up," according to W. C. Fields, "another dollar a quart."

Notice the lowercase *a* in the word "another" in the example above; the first quoted word following an interruption is capitalized only if it begins a new sentence.

Either caps or lowercase are acceptable in numbered or outlined material, but whichever you choose, be consistent.

Can the committee decide (a) when to meet again? (b) what topics to address?

1. Parts of Speech	*or*	1. Parts of Speech
a. noun		a. Noun
b. verb		b. Verb
c. adjective		c. Adjective

Capitalize the first word following a colon only if it begins a complete sentence.

There are two things to aim at in life: First, get what you want; after that, enjoy it.—*Logan Pearsall Smith*

There are three kinds of people: those who can count and those who can't.

Capitalize the first word of a resolution.

Resolved, That proliferation of nuclear weapons be halted...

Titles, Headings, and Legends
Capitalize the first letter of the following:

• First and last words

Pride and Prejudice

- All important words (nouns, pronouns, adjectives, adverbs, verbs, and subordinate conjunctions such as *although, because, since, unless, whether*)

  "I'll Be Seeing You"
  Conditions Following Hurricane Hilda
  Life Down Under: A Visit to Australia
  Legal Aspects of Your Software

- The first word of a hyphenated compound

  Defense Spending Re-examined

- The second word of a hyphenated compound if it's a noun or has the same force as the first word

  Cross-Country Skiing

Do **not** capitalize the first letter of the following:

- Articles (*a, an, the*), unless they are the first word or follow a dash or colon

  How a First Book Became a Best-Seller
  In Search of Funding: A Quick Guide

- Prepositions, unless they are the first or last word or are an inseparable part of a verb

  Wind in the Willows
  For Whom the Bell Tolls
  "Fixing Up a Brownstone"

- The *to* in infinitives

  How to Write a Readable Business Report

- The second word of a hyphenated compound when it modifies the first word or when the words are considered a unit

  The Co-pilot's Handbook
  Free-for-alls in the Nation's Capital

Parts of a Book

Style guides vary in their treatment of parts of a book or literary work: chapter 2 or Chapter 2. I prefer the capitalized version, because Chapter 2 seems like a proper noun (a specific chapter), and proper nouns are capped.

Passing reference to a table of contents, glossary, bibliography, and index appears in lowercase:

  In his introduction, Huxley states...

but cross-references require capitals:

  Additional sources are listed in the Bibliography.

Names and Terms

Capitalize proper names or nouns (names of specific people or places).

  Alexis de Tocqueville
  Alexander the Great
  American Telephone & Telegraph Company
  the Astrodome
  Atlanta Braves
  the Big Apple
  the Biltmore Hotel
  First Lady Martha Washington (the First Lady)

the Los Angeles Music Center
Washington, D.C.
Wild Bill Hickok
William Carlos Williams

Use lowercase for most words derived from proper nouns: arabic numerals, french fries, swiss cheese, venetian blinds, diesel engine, roman numerals, vulcanize, watt, klieg lights.

Capitalize personal titles (professional, religious, military, and civil) that immediately precede a person's name.

President Washington
Chief Justice Peter Mendosa
General Manager Sellars
Admiral Lesley Chang
Rabbi Weiss
The Reverend Audrey McIntosh

Use lowercase when such titles are part of an appositive.

Reade A. Seymour, superintendent of schools,
Susan Ferraro, chief horticulturist,
Andrew Washington, professor of astronomy,
Malcolm R. Keynes, president of the United States,
the president of XYZ Corporation, Robert S. Barron,
Canadian prime minister, Bernadette Bayer,
the governor of Nebraska, Frank Meyers,

Also note the following usage:

the President, the Vice President (when referring to the incumbent U.S. official)
the presidential yacht

the dean's office, the Dean's List

Rhodes scholar

Pardon me, Governor, will you make a statement?

The president of Techniplex will visit the company's Texas
plant next week.

Geopolitical Terms

Capitalize words such as *state*, *avenue*, *city*, or *valley* when they
follow and are part of a specific name. Use lowercase when
they precede the name or stand alone.

the Australian Outback, the Outback

the East, West, North, South (U.S.)

eastern time zone, southern accent, west of town, south of
the border

the equator, the Equatorial Current

the Gulf Stream

Long Island, a Caribbean island

New York City, the city of New York

Palos Verdes Peninsula (the proper name of a town), *but* the
San Francisco peninsula (a general description)

the Province of Quebec, the province

the Republican party, the Democrats, the Labor government

Southern Hemisphere

southern Texas, upstate New York

the Stone Age, the Jurassic period

Tenth Congressional District

the Versailles Treaty, the treaty of Versailles

Washington State, the state of Washington

the White House

Lowercase a plural generic term when it follows more than one name.

the John Hancock and Empire State buildings
the Missouri and Ohio rivers

Capitalize generic terms that precede more than one name.

Mounts McKinley and Rainier
Lakes Onandaga and Cayuga

Organizations, Institutions, Companies

Center for Defense Information
Girl Scouts
Humane Society
Periwinkle Press
Scripps Institution
Society for the Preservation of Barber-Shop Quartets
Stanford University

Calendar

Capitalize days of the week, months, and holidays (President's Day, Fourth of July). For A.M. and P.M., use small caps, if available; otherwise use lowercase: a.m., p.m.

Lowercase seasons (spring, fall) and time zones (central daylight time, Pacific standard time).

Religious Terms

Allah, Buddha, Elohim, Holy Father, Jesus Christ, the Messiah, Mohammed, the Supreme Being, Mater Dolorosa, Ayotollah

Old Testament, the Koran, King James Version, Dead Sea Scrolls

Gnosticism, Sufi, Baha'i Faith, Presbyterian, Seventh-day Adventist

Ark of the Covenant, Garden of Eden, Ecce Homo, the Diaspora, the Crusades, the Hegira, the Inquisition

Scientific Terms

Genus is capitalized, species lowercased; both are set in italic type.

Homo sapiens

Larger divisions (phylum, class, order, family) are capitalized and set in roman type.

Chordata
Primates

English words derived from the scientific terms are lowercased.

primates
omnivores

Only proper names that are part of a medical term or physical law are capitalized.

Rhys' syndrome
Faraday's constant
Hodgkin's disease

The names of chemical elements and compounds are lower-cased when written out and capitalized when appearing as chemical symbols.

sodium chloride   NaCl

Trademarks

The *Chicago Manual of Style* says a "reasonable effort" should be made to capitalize products that are protected by trademarks: Seven-Up, Tylenol, Teflon, Kleenex, Xerox. Unless you have a reason for promoting a trademarked product, use generic terms: adhesive bandage, instead of Band-Aid; photocopy, instead of Xerox. On the other hand, whoever heard of an adhesive-bandage solution?

Military Terms

82nd Airborne Division
98th Field Artillery
the Allies, the Union soldiers, the Rebels, the Red Coats
    Army headquarters
Napoleonic Wars
Purple Heart
Sergeant William Posner, the sergeant
Seventh Fleet, the fleet
United States Navy, the navy, the U.S. Navy, the U.S.S.
    New Jersey, Arkansas National Guard, the guard
Victoria Cross
War of 1812

Computer Terminology

Writers in the field of computers are developing their own rules of style. Acronyms abound (SCSI, BIOS). Computer functions are given initial caps (Enter; Find and Replace), while computer languages appear either with initial caps (Java) or all caps (COBOL). Compounds are treated as one word (laptop, backup), hyphenated (hand-held), and two words (screen saver). Caps pop up in the middle of some compounds (ScanDisk, FlameThrower); hyphens are found in e-commerce, but not in eFilter.

To some extent, you can write your own rules. The overriding considerations are consistency and ease of understanding. Keep track of the choices you make on a style sheet (see p. 24).

Numbers

The following rules will help you decide whether to express numbers as figures (1, 2, 3) or words (one, two, three).

In business or technical writing or in journalism, use words for numbers 1 through 9; use figures for 10 or above.

> There were three applicants for the job.
> There were 12 applicants for the job.

In writing with a literary flavor, the dividing point is 100 instead of 10.

If a sentence or paragraph has related numbers that are both above and below 10, write the related numbers as figures.

> The three lines had 9, 12, and 15 applicants.
> (**Three** is not related to the other numbers and thus follows the previous rule.)

Spell out numbers that begin a sentence; if a related number appears in the same sentence, write it as a word, too.

> Fifty million Frenchmen can't be wrong.

> Twenty members voted yes; fifteen voted no. (*Not* Twenty members voted yes; 15 voted no.)

> One dollar out of every ten earned goes into health care.

Express large numbers in figures or in mixed figure-word form, but be consistent.

> $10,000,000 or $10 million
> 5.7 billion
> 3-1/2 million

Use figures for dates, as follows:

> July 4, 1776 *or* 4 July 1776
> 7/4/76 *or* 7/4/1776 (U.S.)
> 4/7/76 *or* 4/7/1776 (U.K.)

Because of the confusion that might result from the numbered form, writing the month as a word is preferred.

Use figures with units of time or measurement.

10 a.m., 9 o'clock
32 degrees Fahrenheit
2 half-gallons
$^1/_2$-inch pipe
20 kilometers
3-$^1/_2$ yards
3-foot ruler
1 x 8 inches
8-$^1/_2$ by 11 inch paper
55 MPH
35-mm camera
a 40-hour week, *but* forty 50-cent stamps

Use figures in the following cases:

a vote of 5 to 4
a score of 14-0
a 3-for-1 stock split
divide by 2
an increase of 4.65
50 cents
a population of 10,372
Suite 1152

Use words in the following cases:

thousands of refugees
losses in the millions
twelve hundred words

a population of about fifty thousand
one-half of the work force
in their sixties *or* in their 60s

Commas

Americans and British use commas to separate long numbers into groups of three digits (10,576,435). The European practice calls for spaces or periods (4 000 000 or 4.000.000).

Companies often have a style manual that dictates whether to use commas in a four-digit number that appears in the text (3,500 or 3500). In all cases, alignment of tabular matter requires commas when there are four or more digits.

```
 3,500
17,100
   619
 6,800
```

Commas are not used in the following:

- Page numbers (p. 1142)

- Serial numbers (73027894WG)

- Radio frequency (1330 kilocycles)

- To the right of the decimal point (1.53858)

Spelling

Misspelled words in business letters or manuscripts present your message in a flawed way. They also increase the likelihood of your being misunderstood and suggest that you are too lazy to use a dictionary.

Becoming a good speller is largely a matter of attitude. Once you are convinced that correct spelling is important, you will find the moments needed to look up and memorize difficult words. Make a list of the words that give you the most trouble, and update it as you master each one.

If a dictionary lists a second spelling, separated from the main entry by a comma or the word *or*, both spellings are considered acceptable (*ax, axe*). If the second spelling is separated by a period and introduced by the word *Also*, the main entry is preferred (*esophagus*.... Also *oesophagus*).

The following guidelines focus on some of the most common spelling problems.

Suffixes

-ance or -ence. When the final *c* or *g* has a soft sound, use *-ence*, *-ent*, or *-ency*.

> obsolescence, magnificent, emergency, indigent

When the final *c* or *g* has a hard sound, use *-ance*, *-ant*, or *-ancy*.

> significant, extravagance

-able or -ible. Words that have an *-ation* form usually take *-able*.

> dispensable (dispensation)
> irritable (irritation)
> quotable (quotation)
> imaginable (imagination)

Words that have an *-ive*, *-tion*, *-sion*, or *-id* form usually take *-ible*.

> combustible (combustion)
> reversible (reversion)
> collectible (collective)
> digestible (digestion)

Exceptions: definable (definition), sensible (sensation)

-ceed, -cede, or -sede. Three words end with *-ceed* and one with *-sede*.

> exceed
> proceed
> succeed
> supersede

All others ending in this syllable are spelled *-cede*: accede, concede, precede, secede, etc.

-ize or -ise. In general, this verb suffix is spelled *-ize* in the United States (ostracize, sterilize) and *-ise* in the U.K. (ostracise, sterilise). However, the preferred spelling in the U.S. of the following words is *-ise*.

> advertise
> chastise
> exorcise
> franchise

Adding Suffixes

When a word ends in a silent *e*, drop the *e* if the suffix begins with a vowel.

> dance, dancing
> make, making
> smile, smiling
> use, usable

Exceptions: mileage, shoeing, and words ending in a soft *c* or *g* (enforceable, manageable).

Retain the silent *e* if the suffix begins with a consonant.

> grate, grateful
> late, lately

Exceptions: abridgment, acknowledgment, awful, judgment, wholly, wisdom, and such words as duly and argument, in which the silent *e* is immediately preceded by a vowel other than *e*.

When a word ends in *ie*, change the *i* to y and drop the *e*.

die, dying
lie, lying

When a word ending in y is preceded by a vowel, retain the y.

buy, buyer
destroy, destroyer
enjoy, enjoyment

Exceptions: daily, gaiety, laid, paid, said

If the y is preceded by a consonant, change the y to *i*.

body, bodily
dry, drier (i.e., more dry)
happy, happiness
hazy, hazier

Exceptions: fryer, dryer (an appliance), and others formed from one-syllable words such as shy and wry; also, the words baby, lady, and the suffixes -ship (ladyship) and -like (city-like).

When a root word ends with a consonant that is preceded by a single vowel and the suffix begins with a vowel, double the consonant.

control, controlled
forget, forgetting
occur, occurrence
program, programmer
refer, referred
regret, regrettable

remit, remittance
transfer, transferring

Exceptions: buses, busing, transferable, and words where the accent moves from the last syllable to a preceding one (prefer, preference).

Do not double the final consonant in the following cases:

- If the suffix begins with a consonant

  commit, commitment

- If the final consonant is preceded by more than one vowel

  congeal, congealed

- If the word is accented on any syllable except the last

  bias, biased

Exceptions: handicapped, monogrammed, outfitter.

When the word ends in *c*, add a *k* in order to retain the hard sound.

mimicking
picnicking
politicking
shellacked

Plurals

Most nouns are made plural by adding s.

alibis	paths
beliefs	plaintiffs
locks	values

But if the word ends in *s*, *x*, *ch*, *sh*, *z* or *j*, add *es*.

    trenches
    bushes
    dresses
    boxes
    waltzes

If a noun ending in *y* is preceded by a consonant, change the *y* to *i* and add *es*.

    cities
    levies
    countries
    stories
    families

Note: Proper names ending in *y* usually retain the *y* in their plural form.

    two hot Julys
    the Ogilvys

Exceptions: the Rockies, the Alleghenies

Some nouns that end in *f*, *ff*, or *fe* are made plural by changing the *f* to *v* and adding *es*.

    knives
    shelves
    halves
    lives

Some of these have two forms.

scarves, scarfs
loaves, loafs
wharves, wharfs

Some nouns ending in *f* do not change when made plural.

chefs
chiefs

If a noun ending in *o* is preceded by a vowel, add *s*.

cameos
ratios
studios
zoos

If the *o* is preceded by a consonant, an *es* is often added.

tomatoes
echoes
torpedoes
heroes

Some of the more than 40 exceptions to this rule are silos, commandos, mementos, and musical terms such as solos, banjos, and pianos.

Some nouns have the same form for singular and plural.

sheep
deer
corps
scissors
remains
offspring

Some nouns change internally to indicate the plural form.

tooth, teeth
mouse, mice
woman, women

Hard-to-Spell Words

Many difficult words simply have to be memorized, but this is not hard to do. You soon develop a sense of whether a word "looks right." When in doubt, look it up.

The following words frequently show up on lists of spelling bugaboos.

accommodate
accumulate
acknowledgment
all right
consensus
embarrass
existence
harass
inoculate
irrelevant
judgment
liaison
lightning
maintenance
maneuver
miscellaneous
parallel
prerogative

pseudonym
recommend
renaissance
rhythm
surprise
weird

Quotations

Capitalize the first word in a quotation, unless an ellipsis (...) indicates that the quotation begins in mid-sentence.

> "It's bad to suppress laughter," Fred Allen once said, adding that "it goes right back down and spreads to your hips."

In legal or scholarly writing, use brackets to show where you have added a word or capital letter.

> The history of our time is a history of phrases, which rise to great power and then suddenly pass away: "the merchants of death,"... "America first," "cash and carry,"... "bring the boys home,"... [F]ew men have had either the courage or the resources to stand up to these shibboleths.—*Russell Davenport*

With quotations of more than one paragraph, you have two choices.

- Place quotation marks at the beginning of each paragraph but at the end of only the final paragraph.

- Indent the quotation as a block and use no quotation marks.

Do not use quotation marks in the following cases:

> Charles Dudley Warner observed that the thing generally raised on city land is taxes.

> The question remained, Who was responsible?

> Samuel Clemens, better known as Mark Twain...

> The so-called gender gap has taken on political overtones. (not the so-called "gender gap")

> Learning when to say No is an important lesson in business.

Word Division

A word processor does a good job of dividing words at the right-hand margin, so I've included only a few rules.

Word Division Do's

Divide between syllables, according to pronunciation.

> market-able, *not* mar-ketable
> dis-tant, *not* dist-ant

Divide between two consonants that are surrounded by vowels.

> mas-ter
> phar-macy
> sur-vey
> sus-tain

Divide at prefixes or suffixes that contain three or more letters.

> pre-ven-tion
> super-market

infra-red
contra-band
mother-hood
pseudo-science

Divide between doubled consonants unless they are at the end of the root word.

com-mit-tee
book-keeper
but-ter
can-non
recur-ring
swim-ming
run-ning
plan-ning
forestall-ing

Word Division Don'ts

Don't divide one-syllable words.

thought
screamed
lounge
noise
burned
dumped

Don't divide one-letter syllables.

omen, *not* o-men
alive, *not* a-live
folio, *not* foli-o

Don't divide in such a way that you create a misleading pronunciation.

> dancing, *not* danc-ing
> pred-ator, *not* pre-dator
> subtle, *not* sub-tle
> hoping, *not* hop-ing

Don't carry a two-letter syllable over to the next line.

> leader, *not* lead-er
> fainted, *not* faint-ed

Don't separate abbreviations and figures.

> 200 B.C., *not* 200/B.C.
> 1:00 a.m., *not* 1:00/a.m.
> 150 km, *not* 150/km

Try to avoid dividing personal names, but if necessary, break after the middle initial.

> Julia E./Pascuale
> M. V./Thomas

Don't separate the elements of an outline or list, such as (a) or (1), from what follows them; carry such marks over to the next line.

> **Wrong:** The program to redevelop the inner city will include (a) an environmental impact report, (b) sources of funding...

> **Right:** The program to redevelop the inner city will include (a) an environmental impact report, (b) sources of...

Don't divide the last word of more than two consecutive lines.

Don't divide the last word of a paragraph or the last word on a right-hand page.

Document Integrity

Seemingly trivial errors in assembling a document distract the reader's attention from your ideas. A document may be 99 percent error-free, but the 1 percent with errors is what's noticed.

The changes made during editing increase the chance of a mismatch between parts of a document. Gaps in numbering, missing figures or tables, and discrepancies between the table of contents and text are typical slipups. Edit for this kind of integrity with a separate pass through a document, checking the following elements.

Numbering

Are pages, sections, and chapters numbered sequentially? Are cross-references correct? Are references to other documents numbered sequentially and listed in that order in a bibliography?

Figures and Tables

Are figures and tables numbered sequentially? Is the numbering style consistent (e.g., arabic or roman numerals, hyphenation, decimals)? Is the format and style of captions uniform? Are the titles or captions of any figures or tables identical? If so, change one of them so that readers can distinguish between them. Did you misplace a modifier in a caption?

> Shirley Hansen greets her family after three years in O'Hare Airport.

Table of Contents
Does the text for all of the headings cited in the table of contents still exist? Are the headings correctly worded? Are the page numbers correct?

Page Layouts
Do running heads (chapter or section titles that appear at the top of each page) match the text? Are numbered footnotes sequential?

Parallelism
Is every subparagraph (a) followed by subparagraph (b)? Is (i) followed by (ii)?

Document Appearance
A reader's first impression of what you have written is visual. Keep the goal of a pleasing presentation in mind as you make decisions about the appearance of a document.

Spacing is key. Information is more readily absorbed if it isn't too densely packed, so create plenty of white space around your words.

Indented portions of text and bulleted information are eye-catching, and an outline format is occasionally useful to emphasize the organization of your material.

Should you add chapter headings? Section headings or footings? They can help the reader find a specific part of a long document. Location of page numbers is another variable; try several locations and decide.

Are the page breaks satisfactory? Printers advise you to avoid the following "bad breaks."

- Short line at the top of a page (called a *widow*)

- Heading at the bottom of a page (at least two lines of text should follow a heading)

- A page that ends with a hyphenated word (some accept such a break on a left-hand page)

- A quoted portion that begins on the last line or ends on the first line of a page (at least two lines of the quotation should appear in either place)

- A footnote that is not on the same page as its original citation (if the first two lines are on the same page, the footnote can be continued on the following page)

Desktop publishing software comes loaded with options: justified margins, a wide variety of fonts and sizes, italic and boldface type, multiple columns, drop caps, and so on. The type of document (or in-house policy) may determine these choices.

As you examine the final document, divorce yourself from its content and consider only its visual impact. Although you want to take advantage of the opportunities for adding graphic interest to text, keep in mind that ease of reading comes first. The reader should not have to struggle to see text that's overlaid on graphics or printed in eye-catching colors that reduce legibility. Graphic images should complement text, not compete with it.

> Nothing you write, if you hope to be good, will ever come out as you first hoped.—*Lillian Hellman*

Good writing comes from good rewriting. It's a dynamic process that presents challenges and provides satisfactions whenever you put words together. I hope you find *Rewrite Right!* a helpful guide along the way.

Glossary

Adjective. A word that describes or limits the meaning of a noun or noun phrase.

> Niagara Falls is simply a <u>vast, unnecessary</u> amount of water going the wrong way and then falling over <u>unnecessary</u> rocks.—*Oscar Wilde*

Adverb. A word that modifies or expands the meaning of a verb, adjective, or other adverb.

> ...There is no <u>distinctively</u> native American criminal class except Congress.—*Mark Twain*

Alliteration. The use of words that begin with or contain the same letter or sound, in order to achieve a certain effect.

> Finding Facts Fast
> Write Right! A Desk Drawer Digest...

Antecedent. The word, phrase, or clause referred to by a pronoun. Skilled writers avoid ambiguous antecedents. See p. 55 and p. 124.

> I'm a great believer in <u>luck</u>, and I find that the harder
> antecedent
> I work, the more I have of <u>it</u>.—*Thomas Jefferson*
> pronoun

Antonym. A word having a meaning opposite to the meaning of another word. See Synonym.

> slow/fast
> hot/cold
> difficult/easy

Appositive. A noun or phrase that identifies the preceding word or concept.

> Gabriel Garcia Marquez, the Nobel laureate,...
> my supervisor, Jack Campbell,...

Article. The words *a, an,* and *the.* Usually classified as adjectives.

Case. The inflection or change made to a pronoun in order to show its relation to other words. Pronouns in the **nominative** case are subjects of verbs (*we*); in the **objective** case pronouns are objects of verbs or prepositions (*us*); and in the **possessive** case pronouns show possession (*our*). See p. 121.

> <u>We</u> gave <u>them</u> <u>our</u> answer.

We is the subject of the verb *gave*, *them* is its indirect object, and *our* shows possession of the noun *answer*.

Clause. A group of words that contains a subject and predicate. An **independent** clause expresses a complete thought. A **dependent** (subordinate) clause does not express a complete thought and depends on the main (independent) clause to complete its meaning.

> If you aren't fired with enthusiasm,
> dependent clause
> you will be fired with enthusiasm.—*Vince Lombardi*
> independent clause

A **restrictive** clause is necessary to define or limit the word it modifies; it is not set off by commas.

> My clothes are addressed to women
> who can afford to travel with forty suitcases.
> restrictive clause
> —*Yves Saint Laurent*

A **nonrestrictive** clause adds information but does not limit what it modifies; it is set off by commas.

> To say nothing, especially when speaking,
> nonrestrictive clause
> is half the art of diplomacy.—*Will and Ariel Durant*

Cliché. An expression that has become dull and unoriginal by overuse.

> Clichés should be avoided like the plague.

Complement. A word or phrase that completes the meaning of the verb.

The judge named Sanchez <u>jury foreman</u>.

We found their argument <u>unconvincing</u>.

Happiness is <u>having a scratch for every itch</u>.—*Ogden Nash*

Compound. Consisting of two or more elements.

How can one conceive of a <u>one-party</u> system in a country
compound adjective
that has over two hundred varieties of cheese?
—*Charles deGaulle*

<u>The wisdom of the wise and the experience of the ages</u>
compound subject
are perpetuated by quotations.—*Benjamin Disraeli*

I <u>hate and regret</u> the failure of my marriages.
compound verb
—*J. Paul Getty*

Compound words are classified as temporary, permanent, open, and closed. A **temporary** compound consists of words joined by the writer for a momentary purpose.

Love is <u>a many-splintered</u> thing.—*R. Buckminster Fuller*

A **permanent** compound can be found in the dictionary, indicating its acceptance in our language: half-breed. An **open** compound is written as two separate words: cash crop. Write a **closed** compound as a single word: casework, paycheck.

Conjunction. A word that connects words, phrases, and clauses. **Coordinating** conjunctions (*and*, *but*, *or*, *nor*, *for*, *yet*, and *so*) connect elements of equal rank.

nuts and bolts
Tom, Dick, or Harry

Two independent clauses are joined by a coordinating conjunction.

Music is my mistress, and she plays second fiddle to no one.—*Duke Ellington*

Coordinating conjunctions used in pairs are called **correlatives**:

either/or
not only/but also
both/and

Subordinating conjunctions (*that*, *when*, *where*, *while*, *if*, *because*, *although*, *since*, etc.) connect elements of unequal rank (i.e., an independent and a dependent clause).

A man in love is incomplete <u>until</u> he has married. Then he's finished.—*Zsa Zsa Gabor*

Contraction. The use of an apostrophe to indicate omitted letters or numbers.

can't (cannot)
'50 (1950)

Dangling modifier. A modifier that cannot logically modify any word in a sentence. See p. 127.

> Having left in a hurry, his wallet was still on the dresser.

Gerund. A verb form that ends in *-ing* and is used as a noun. See Participle.

> <u>Multitasking</u> is efficient.

> <u>Writing</u> is the hardest way of <u>earning</u> a <u>living</u>, with the possible exception of <u>wrestling</u> alligators.—*Olin Miller*

Infinitive. The word *to* plus the present tense of a verb.

> In a hierarchy every employee tends <u>to rise</u> to his level of incompetence.—*Laurence Peter*

In a **split** infinitive, a word or phrase comes between *to* and the verb.

> **Split:** They were asked to promptly complete the questionnaire.

> **Improved:** They were asked to complete the questionnaire promptly.

> **Acceptable:** We expect to more than double sales next year.

Inflection. Changes in the form of a word to show grammatical functions such as case, voice, person, mood, tense, and number. Thus, inflection of the pronoun *I* to *we* shows the change from singular to plural; inflection of *I* to *me* shows the change from nominative to objective case.

Interjection. A word or phrase that expresses strong feelings; an exclamation.

> My word!
> Ouch!
> Not on your life!
> Cool!

Metaphor. The implicit comparison of concepts by substituting one concept for another in order to suggest their similarity. "The dawn of civilization" indirectly compares dawn to the early days of civilization. "The long arm of the law" gives law a human body in order to illustrate a similarity of function. See p. 84.

> Writing, like life itself, is a voyage of discovery.—*Henry Miller*

Misplaced modifier. Incorrect placement of a modifier, which produces a misleading meaning. See p. 126.

> **Misplaced:** Over one million Americans have a heart attack every year.

> **Correct:** Every year over one million Americans have a heart attack.

Mood. The change made in a verb to show whether it makes a statement (**indicative** mood), is a command (**imperative** mood), or expresses a condition contrary to fact (**subjunctive** mood). See p. 130.

Noun. A word that names things. "Things" can be physical objects (table, pen), abstract concepts (humor, truth), actions (writing, scratching), substances (air, water), measures (centimeter, inch), places (street, factory), persons (reporter, mechanic), and so on. **Proper** nouns refer to a specific person, place, or thing (Michelangelo, Houston, World War II); they are capitalized.

Parallel construction. Using grammatically parallel forms (e.g., infinitives or nouns) to emphasize the similarity or relatedness of ideas.

> Unparallel: The power to tax involves the power of destruction.

> Parallel: The power to tax involves the power to destroy. —*John Marshall*

Participle. A verb form used as an adjective. See Gerund.

> an <u>inspiring</u> lecture
> a <u>worn</u> collar
> the <u>outraged</u> electorate
> a <u>frozen</u> dessert
> The <u>debugging</u> procedure took only a few minutes.

Parts of speech. The classification of words according to the function they perform in a sentence: noun, pronoun, verb, adjective, adverb, preposition, conjunction, and interjection. The definition of each part of speech appears at its alphabetical entry.

Person. The speaker is the first person (*I*, *we*), the person spoken to is the second person (*you*), and the person or thing spoken of is the third person (*he*, *she*, *they*, *it*).

Phrase. A group of words that has no subject or predicate and that functions as if it were a single word.

> Turn right <u>at the signal</u>.
> prepositional phrase

> <u>Knowing the subject thoroughly</u>, she was quick to reply.
> participial phrase

Predicate. A group of words that makes a statement or asks a question about the subject of a sentence. A **simple** predicate consists of a verb; a **complete** predicate includes verbs, modifiers, objects, and complements.

> A student <u>can win twelve letters at a university without learning how to write one</u>.—*Robert Maynard Hutchins*

Prefix. A word element that is placed in front of a root word, thereby changing or modifying the meaning.

> <u>re</u>claim
> <u>mis</u>print
> <u>macro</u>cosm
> <u>un</u>easy

Preposition. A word that shows the relationship between a noun and the object of the preposition. In the sentence "She put the check in the envelope," *in* is the preposition that shows the relationship between the noun *check* and the object of the preposition *envelope*.

> The buck stops with the guy who signs the checks.—*Rupert Murdoch*

By the way, a preposition is a fine thing to end a sentence with. ☺

Pronoun. A word that takes the place of a noun and is used in order to avoid cumbersome repetition. See p. 121. **Personal** pronouns include *I, you, he, she, it* (sing.), *we, you, they* (pl.), and their inflected forms (e.g., *me, her, them, ours*).

> The very fact that <u>we</u> make such a to-do over golden weddings indicates <u>our</u> amazement at human endurance. The celebration is more in the nature of a reward for stamina. —*Ilka Chase*

Relative pronouns (*who, which, that,* and compounds like *whoever*) relate one part of a sentence to a word in another part.

> A government <u>that</u> robs Peter to pay Paul can always depend on the support of Paul.—*G. B. Shaw*

Indefinite pronouns include *any, some, each, every,* and compounds with *-body* and *-one,* such as *no one, everyone, somebody,* and *nobody*.

> Experience is the name <u>everyone</u> gives to their mistakes. —*Oscar Wilde*

Reflexive and **intensive** pronouns include *myself, themselves,* and others formed by adding *-self* or *-selves* to a personal pronoun.

Tact is the ability to describe others as they see them-selves.—*Abraham Lincoln*

Demonstrative pronouns include *this*, *that*, *these*, and *those*.

That is the wrong answer.

Interrogative pronouns include *who*, *which*, and *what*.

Who shall guard the guardians themselves?—*Juvenal*

Sentence. A combination of words that contains at least one subject and predicate (grammatical definition); a group of words that expresses a complete thought (popular definition). Sentence structures are classified as simple, compound, and complex.

A **simple** sentence is one independent clause consisting of a subject and predicate; the sentence may have modifying phrases but no dependent clauses.

There is no abstract art. You must always start with some-thing.—*Pablo Picasso*

A **compound** sentence is two or more independent clauses.

Blessed are the young, for they shall inherit the national debt.—*Herbert Hoover*

A **complex** sentence is one independent and one or more dependent clauses.

When ideas fail, words come in very handy.—*Johann Goethe*

Power and violence are opposites; where one rules absolutely, the other is absent.—*Hannah Arendt*

Sentence functions are categorized as declarative, interrogative, imperative, and exclamatory. A **declarative** sentence makes an assertion.

> Success is simply a matter of luck. Ask any failure.—*Earl Wilson*

An **interrogative** sentence asks a question.

> How can they tell?—*Dorothy Parker, on hearing of Calvin Coolidge's death*

An **imperative** sentence issues a command.

> Don't trust anyone over thirty!—*Mario Savio*

An **exclamatory** sentence expresses a strong feeling.

> America is a mistake—a giant mistake!—*Sigmund Freud*

Sentence faults result from trying to crowd too much into a sentence (a **run-on**) or from failing to have enough in a sentence (a **fragment**). A run-on is two independent clauses joined only by a comma (called a **comma splice**):

> **Comma Splice:** We are temporarily out of widgets, however we expect a shipment within two weeks.

> **Correct:** We are temporarily out of widgets; however, we expect a shipment within two weeks.

or two independent clauses with no punctuation connecting them (called a **fused sentence**):

> **Fused Sentence:** We expect immediate payment otherwise we will turn your account over to a collection agency.

Correct: We expect immediate payment; otherwise, we will turn your account over to a collection agency.

A fragment is a partial sentence that either lacks a verb or fails to express a complete thought.

Wrong: Whenever I think I know all the answers.

Right: Whenever I think I know all the answers, life asks a few more questions.

Fragments are acceptable in questions and answers, for occasional emphasis ("Not likely."), in transitions ("On to the next point."), and in definitions. See p. 133.

Simile. A direct comparison using the word *like* or *as*. See p. 84.

Having a family is like having a bowling alley installed in your brain.—*Martin Mull*

Suffix. A word element added to the end of a root word.

geno<u>cide</u>
bore<u>dom</u>
forti<u>fy</u>
back<u>ward</u>

Synonym. A word similar in meaning to another word. See Antonym.

hazard/danger
invisible/unseen
handbook/manual

Tense. The form of a verb that shows distinctions in time: present, past, future, present perfect, past perfect, future perfect. See p. 128.

Verb. A word that asserts that something exists, has certain characteristics, or acts in a certain way. Verbs change form to indicate time (she will speak, he spoke), person (I speak, he speaks), or mood (Speak!). See p. 128.

Linking verbs, such as *to be, to appear, to become,* and *to seem,* serve as connections between the subject and its complement. (See Complement.)

> Pollution <u>is</u> nothing but resources we're not harvesting.
> —*R. Buckminster Fuller*

Transitive verbs require a direct object to complete their meaning.

> Big girls <u>need</u> big diamonds.—*Margaux Hemingway*

Intransitive verbs do not require an object.

> Society attacks early when the individual is helpless.
> —*B. F. Skinner*

Voice. The form of the verb used to express the relation between the subject and the action expressed by the verb. In the *passive voice,* the subject is acted upon; in the *active voice,* the subject performs the action. See p. 77.

> **Passive:** The tie-breaker was won by Marisela.

> **Active:** Marisela won the tie-breaker.

Index